TWENTIETH CENTURY CANADIAN COMPOSERS

Twentieth Century
Canadian Composers

Volume One

Ian L. Bradley
University of Victoria

Acknowledgements

For permission to reprint copyrighted material, grateful acknowledgement is made to the following publishers, authors, composers, and agents:

Murray Adaskin for *Diversion for Orchestra, Rondino for Nine Instruments, Sonata for Violin and Piano,* and *Prairie Lily.*

Berandol Music Limited, 11 St. Joseph Street, Toronto, Ontario for *Altitude* © 1961 (BER1438), *String Quartet* © 1974 (BER1096), and *Symphonie gaspésienne* (manuscript, rental) by Claude Champagne; *Images* by Harry Freedman; *Psalm 150* by Jean Papineau-Couture; *Threnody,* and *Epitaph for Moonlight* by R. Murray Schafer; *Opening Night* — A Theatre Overture, and *Variations and Toccata* by Robert Turner; and *Piano Concerto in C Minor* © 1960 (BER1464) by Healey Willan.

Harry Freedman for *Variations,* and *The Wind and the Rain.*

The Frederick Harris Music Co. Limited, 529 Speers Road, Oakville, Ontario for *An Apostrophe to the Heavenly Hosts* by Healey Willan.

Jaymar Music, Box 3083, London, Ontario for *String Quartet in C Minor* by Sir Ernest MacMillan.

Leeds Music Limited, Canada for *Tangents* by Harry Freedman; and *Divertimento No. 3* and *Divertimento No. 5* by John Weinzweig.

Oxford University Press, 200 Madison Avenue, New York, N.Y. 10016 *for Two Sketches for String Quartet.*

The Ernest MacMillan Estates *for Concert Overture* by Sir Ernest MacMillan.

Jean Papineau-Couture for *Pièce concertante No. 3,* and *Concerto for Piano and Orchestra.*

C. F. Peters Corporation, 373 Park Avenue South, New York, N.Y. 100016 for *Passacaglia and Fugue No. 2 in E Minor* © 1959 (P6145) by Healey Willan.

G. Ricordi & Company Limited, Canada, 497 Eglinton Avenue West, Toronto, Ontario for *Cantate pour une joie* © 1960, *Divertissement* © 1970, and *Triptyque* © 1963 by Pierre Mecure.

Robert Turner for *Serenade for Woodwind Quartet,* and *The Carrion Crow.*

Universal Edition, London for *String Quartet No. 1* © 1970 by R. Murray Schafer.

John Weinzweig for *Woodwind Quintet,* and *To the Lands Over Yonder.*

Music engraving by Musictype Limited, Goodwood, Ontario.

ISBN 0-88874-052-2

iv

Ian L. Bradley

Ian L. Bradley was born in New Zealand and immigrated to British Columbia, Canada in 1955. He received his teacher training in Auckland, New Zealand, specializing in music education. During the last twenty years he has taught general music to elementary grade children and choral music in both junior and senior high schools. In 1966 he obtained his M.Ed. degree (choral music director) from Western Washington State College. He graduated from the University of British Columbia with a Doctorate in Music Education in 1969. His dissertation dealt with the development of student preferences through an analytical approach to listening to contemporary music. At present he is Assistant Professor in Music Education at the University of Victoria, Victoria, B.C., Canada.

Dr. Bradley is extremely interested and active in assisting music teachers to expand their curricular goals. He has written extensively in provincial, national, and international journals on the development of listening skills, the development of musical creativity, the use of contemporary music, and the inclusion of Canadian content in school music. Of recent years he has conducted many music clinics and in-service workshops for teachers throughout the provinces of British Columbia and Alberta. His recently published *Canadian Music for Schools* together with *A Selected Bibliography of Musical Canadiana* should provide teachers and students with valuable resource materials for classroom use.

The present volume is designed specifically to assist in the understanding and enjoyment of Canadian music. Primarily the biographical sketches and analytical listening materials are the result of several years of research by the author in the design and implementation of Canadian music in both schools and colleges. Both attitudinal and preferential response items indicate that guided listening experiences (and the concomitant skill development associated with exercises of this nature) are gradually becoming recognized as important educational goals in music education. Teachers at all levels of music instruction will welcome the availability of new material for themselves and for the additional references offered for classroom use.

v

Contents

Preface   viii

1. HEALEY WILLAN   1

An Apostrophe to the Heavenly Hosts   6
Pianoforte Concerto in C Minor   8
Passacaglia and Fugue No. 2 in E Minor   11

2. CLAUDE CHAMPAGNE   17

Symphonie gaspésienne   21
Altitude   24
String Quartet   28

3. SIR ERNEST CAMPBELL MACMILLAN   33

String Quartet in C Minor   36
Two Sketches for String Quartet   42
Concert Overture   45

4. MURRAY ADASKIN   49

Sonata for Violin and Piano   53
Rondino for Nine Instruments   59
Diversion for Orchestra   61
The Prairie Lily   63

5. JOHN WEINZWEIG   69

Divertimento No. 3   75
Divertimento No. 5   80
Woodwind Quintet   84
To the Lands over Yonder   90

6. JEAN PAPINEAU-COUTURE — 99

Psaume 150 — 103
Pièce concertante No. 3 — 106 ←
Concerto pour piano et orchestre — 112

7. ROBERT TURNER — 117

Opening Night — A Theatre Overture — 122
Variations and Toccata — 126
Serenade for Woodwind Quintet — 130
The Carrion Crow — 133

8. HARRY FREEDMAN — 139

Images — 144
Variations — 151
Tangents — 156
The Wind and the Rain — 161

9. PIERRE MERCURE — 169

Divertissement — 173
Triptyque — 177
Cantate pour une joie — 180

10. R. MURRAY SCHAFER — 189

Threnody — 194
Epitaph for Moonlight — 200 ←
String Quartet No. 1 — 204

Glossary — 211

Italian Terms — 214

Reference Notes — 216

Bibliography — 218

Discography — 221

Preface

This book is written primarily as a guide to listening, enjoying, and understanding Canadian music. It deals exclusively with the significant contributions of ten composers who represent different regions of Canada, and whose musical achievements and influential leadership are widely recognized.

Culturally, Canada is a young country. However, over the last two or three decades, there has been an amazing growth in the musical arts. Despite this changing scene, there is very little public awareness that musical creativity thrives in Canada. The same could also be said in educational circles — particularly in the schools across the country. Fortunately, this situation is changing. Through such agencies as the Canadian Broadcasting Corporation, the Canada Council, the Canadian League of Composers, and the Canadian Music Centre — all dedicated to encouraging musical growth in Canada — there is, musically speaking, an emerging Canadian identity, together with a substantial development in music as a creative, a performing, and a listening art.

Unfortunately, Canadian music has not received sufficient impetus in the educational field. This is not to minimize the efforts of individual schools, colleges, and universities. However, Canadian music as such has in general received little if any exposure; and not because of a lack of interest — as any music teacher may attest. Students are very willing to perform and listen to music of their own country if given the opportunity. This neglect has been due, in part, to the dearth of instructional media. Teachers and student teachers have been unable to acquire introductory materials that would present and explain many of the new contemporary idioms — to say nothing of the difficult task of obtaining suitable recordings.

Recognizing that an anthology of Canadian composers and their works would be of limited value unless the music were readily available, this series presents a descriptive analysis of works recorded by the CBC, and in most instances included in the Canadian Collection, now available for public and educational use. This material will enable both teachers and individuals to become more familiar with each composer's representative music. The analysis of each work, augmented by the thematic illustrations, should enable teachers and students to listen more perceptively as the recordings are played.

This book serves, therefore, to provide help and guidance to teachers and students seeking an introduction to music written by Canadians. It is not intended as an historical survey and no attempt has been made to differentiate the styles of composers or to categorize their music. The biographical information is intended as a sketch of each composer's life rather than as an authoritative monograph. The specific works chosen for analysis do not necessarily represent the composer's most important works, but will serve as a useful introduction to his music. The intent of the analysis is not to be pedantic but to serve as an aid to the listener as the music is played. Words are no substitute for listening. The description of the various characteristics of the music should aid one's understanding, but the ear must provide the real listening experience.

This book has been planned as a result of the writer's belief that listening to music is a valid and acceptable musical activity which can and does contribute to the development of musicality. The suggested analytical listening experiences have been formulated on the fundamental philosophical base that maintains — even insists — that musical growth depends upon the study of music itself, and upon differentiating the constituent elements that determine its significant expressiveness. That is, a progressively more adequate grasp of musical organization is the very heart of the development of understanding and the deepening of appreciation. The term 'listening' as used in this context does not imply, therefore, a passive submissive attitude. Simply to sit and 'audit sound waves' without perceiving or gaining an understanding of the constituent elements of the music that is being performed is merely to hear the music. This is certainly not perceiving the music aesthetically. Unless the individual is experiencing an intellectual apprehension of the various elements that together constitute the music, much of that which is received through the ear is lost and remains meaningless.

Originally this work was intended solely for use in junior and senior high schools. However, as the work progressed, it became more realistic to think of the material as most helpful for university music students, student teachers, and teachers in the schools; for it is with our young teachers that the hope of educating the young of our country lies. Children and young adults have little prejudice against contemporary music. If we provide guidance and encouragement for them to listen to contemporary Canadian music, the rich musical culture that today remains relatively unknown could become an added source of musical enjoyment.

In addition to the compositions selected for responsive listening activities, examples of vocal music have been included. It is hoped that classroom experiences may include the singing of these selections and create further interest in our contemporary composers. A selected bibliography is included for teachers wishing to find more extensive references. This material may provide additional information and assist in developing curricula in this neglected area of music education.

Ian L. Bradley

HEALEY WILLAN
1880-1968
Composer, Organist, Teacher

Without question, James Healey Willan represents the very best of the English choral tradition transplanted into Canada earlier in this century. Born near London (in Balham, Surrey) on October 12, 1880, he later immigrated to Toronto where he remained to the end of his life. His more than fifty years association with the musical life of his new country made him especially endeared and respected as a Canadian musician. For many years Dr. Willan carried the affectionate title 'Dean of Canadian Composers.' Pretentious as the title may sound today, it was a constant reminder to all that in Willan there was a lifetime of musical leadership extended to those who associated with him either at his beloved St. Mary Magdalene, Toronto, or in his other professional capacities at both the Toronto Conservatory of Music and the Faculty of Music of the University of Toronto, Ontario.

Healey Willan received his early musical education at St. Saviour's Choir School, Eastbourne, on the south coast of England. The young Healey made remarkable progress during the six years he spent under the guidance and musical influence of Dr. Sangster, the organist and choirmaster. At eleven years of age he was often allowed to accompany the church services, and to conduct choir rehearsals with choir boys older than himself. In 1895 Healey Willan's family moved to the cathedral city of St. Alban's, northwest of London. Commuting once a week to London, he continued advanced studies under Dr. William Stevenson Hoyte, organist of the

Church of All Saints, London. At sixteen, he became an Associate of the Royal College of Organists, and two years later, in 1899, he passed the required examinations and became a Fellow of the Royal College of Organists. During this period the young organist held several important positions as a church organist; St. Saviour's Church, St. Alban's, 1897-1900; Christ Church, Wanstead, 1900-1903; and St. John the Baptist Church, Kensington, London, 1903-1913. Throughout these ten years Willan was active as a conductor of the Wanstead Choral Society, the Thalian Operatic Society, and most significantly, achieved a reputation as an authority on plainchant in the vernacular. In 1905 he married Gladys Ellen Hall and later became the father of three sons and one daughter.

Willan left his position in Kensington in 1913 at the invitation of Dr. Vogt of the Toronto Conservatory of Music to become the head of the Theory Department of the Toronto Conservatory. On arrival in Toronto, he was appointed organist and choirmaster at St. Paul's Anglican Church, Toronto. In 1921, he accepted a new appointment to St. Mary Magdalene Church, Toronto, where he remained Musical Director until his death forty-seven years later in 1968. During this long period, he held several important positions in the musical life of Toronto. He was Head of the Theory Department at the Conservatory from 1913-36; Vice-Principal between 1920 and 1936; Professor of Music at the University of Toronto from 1937 until 1950; and University Organist from 1932 until 1964. Numerous other positions such as special lecturer, guest lecturer, adjudicator and guest organist, kept Willan busy and an influential musical figure.

Many honours were bestowed on Willan during his lifetime. He was awarded a Doctorate of Music from the University of Cambridge, England; a Doctorate of Literature from McMaster University; a Doctorate of Literature from the University of Manitoba; a Doctorate of Music from the University of Toronto; and from Queen's University in 1952, a Doctorate of Literature. Perhaps the greatest honour, and certainly one Willan prized most, was the honour bestowed on him in 1956, when the Lord Archbishop of Canterbury conferred the Lambeth Doctorate. Only those who have made an outstanding contribution to church music receive such recognition. Canada also recognized Healey Willan's greatness by awarding a Canada Council Medal in 1961-62, and later in 1967 the Companion of the Order of Canada.

Throughout his eighty years as an active musician, Healey Willan composed music of an exceptionally high calibre. The comprehensive *Healey Willan Catalogue* compiled by Giles Bryant, and published in 1972 by the National Library of Canada, includes titles of all the extant works composed during his lifetime. Totalling close to one thousand in individual titles, there is an incredible variety of musical forms, both vocal and instrumental. A summary of such a prolific output includes large dramatic works for stage, large choral works with orchestra, symphonies, concertos, chamber music, piano, organ, and, of course, many sacred anthems, motets for small and large choirs, and secular and sacred songs. A condensed list of significant and representative compositions was published by Giles Bryant in *Musicanada,* No. 9, March, 1968. The most recent condensed list may be found in *Contemporary Canadian Composers,* published by Oxford University Press in 1975. Altogether more than thirty publishers have included Willan's works in their music catalogues, but inevitably a number of works have remained unpublished. From the complete list certain titles are further underlined for their importance and musical merit.

Among the dramatic works, the *15 Sets of Incidental Music for Hart House Theatre* represent early compositions written when Willan was Musical Director of Hart House in the University of Toronto. During these years (1919-1924) in co-operation with Roy Mitchell, the Director, these pieces were written as incidental music for classical plays. **Transit through Fire**—*1942;* and **Deirdre**—*1945;* are two operas that belong in this category. The latter work, **Deirdre,** was revised by the composer in 1962, and again later in 1965. It is Willan's most ambitious work.

Among the orchestral works, **Symphony No. 2 in C minor**—*1941* (revised 1948); the **Concerto in C minor for Piano and Orchestra**—*1944* (revised 1949); and the **Overture to an Unwritten Comedy**—*1951;* are perhaps the best known and most performed. Each has been recorded and included in the CBC *Canadian Collection.*

With hundreds of titles representing sacred choir music, one hesitates to name significant pieces. However, the anthem, **An Apostrophe to the Heavenly Hosts,** written in 1921 (revised in 1952) for double choir and semi-chorus, and the fourteen settings of the **Missa Brevis** (1928-1963), together with the **Liturgical Motets** published by Oxford University Press and Carl Fischer, represent the choral style and idiomatic expression that is Willan's alone. In a discussion of Willan's choral music published in *Contemporary Canadian Composers* these works are considered to contain the composer's "most lasting contribution to church music."

The organ music of Healey Willan is remarkable for its quality and quantity. No other English speaking member of the British Commonwealth has produced such a fine collection. Whether it be for liturgical or recital use, there are many titles from simple to difficult that are published and available for the church organist. In the Chorale Prelude genre alone there are 97 titles most organists would find extremely useful. Such collections as the **Fugal Trilogy, Rondino Elegy and Chaconne,** and **Passacaglia and Fugue No. 2 in E minor,** make useful recital pieces, or splendid organ preludes preceding the church service.

This short survey should be sufficient for the reader to realize the prolific output of this truly remarkable man. Unfortunately, relatively little of Willan's music is available on commercial recordings. However, there are discs which contain some of his organ works, his choral works, and, in the CBC *Canadian Collection,* his orchestral works. The Festival Singers of Canada have recorded several pieces, which are also obtainable. Despite the lack of recordings, it is safe to say that probably among church musicians, Healey Willan's organ and choral music receives as much if not more exposure than most twentieth century composers. As Giles Bryant has said: "To keep green his memory involves no altruistic labour of love—performing his music will always be a delight to performer and listener alike." And finally, Dr. Willan said of himself: "Music has been my chief delight, and if at any time I have been able to share that delight with others, I am content."

Unlike many composers of Willan's generation whose art reflects the restless spirit and troubled climate of the twentieth century, Willan's music more closely approximates the classical traditions. Concerning his musical style the composer said of himself: "It is one of my faults that I have not kept up very well with today's musical developments. But for many years my free time, away from my lecturing, has been devoted to writing music for choirs. You might say I have been steeped in Tudor tradition." Willan's knowledge and love of plainsong dates back to his childhood when he first heard plainchant in the Church of St. George in Beckenham, England. Later, as a young man, he became a friend and associate of Francis Burgess, the founder of the Gregorian Association. The ideals and aspirations of this association are reflected in the works and style of the composer. His use of modality, his flexible rhythmic freedom, and his flowing melismatic passages eventually become an essential part of the later polyphony one finds in the liturgical works. His organ works reflect this influence also. The individual melodic lines retain a characteristic ability to 'sing', and one is conscious of the composer's ability to think vocally and to compose music that is essentially contrapuntal.

For a composer who has over five hundred works published, it seems appropriate to make a number of observations. Many of these works written specifically for the church service are cast in traditional forms; chorales, preludes, arias, passacaglias and fugues, and preludes and fugues. Not all his music is in miniature. Willan's **Introduction, Passacaglia and Fugue** — 1916, is one of the most important organ works of our time. Andrée Desautels quotes the eminent French composer and organist Joseph Bonnet as saying: "This piece is the greatest organ work since J.S. Bach," adding the observation that, "Few musicians can pride themselves on having received such ultimate praise." Dr. Francis Jackson, the distinguished recital organist of York Minster, England, has recorded no less than ten works on Columbia disc MS 6798, which amply illustrate a variety of Willan's organ compositions in addition to the previously mentioned **Introduction, Passacaglia and Fugue.** Other individual selections for organ may also be found in current record catalogues. For the church organist of modest ability, many fine works have been written on plainsong, and well known hymn-tunes, providing a wide variety of interesting literature that is of excellent quality.

One would suspect a man in his late eighties to be quietly retiring from his labours. Not so Healey Willan. His activities, even up to the last few months of his life,

4

would have given pause to a man many years his junior. Engaged in proof-reading the 580 page orchestral score of his opera **Deirdre** he composed the official **Canadian Centennial Anthem,** wrote a **Centennial March** for orchestra or band, took an active part as the subject of a CBC television programme, was involved in the preparation of the CBC Radio performance of his musical pageant **Brébeuf,** and presented three choral-organ recitals with his church choirs!

Of the several Canadian composers included in this series, Willan is undoubtedly the most prolific. His music is also the most traditional in its style and construction. No apology is offered. Willan's music must be considered for its own intrinsic musical merit, and for our purposes, will stand more often in complete contrast to the more avant-garde music of the younger generations of Canadian composers. The three works chosen for listening will illustrate differing genres and musical forms. **An Apostrophe to the Heavenly Hosts** is recorded and available to the public, as is the CBC recording of the composer's **Concerto in C minor for Piano and Orchestra.** A recent recording by the Canadian organist Frederick Geoghegan playing Willan's **Passacaglia and Fugue No. 2 in E minor** is also obtainable. This work should most adequately illustrate in some measure the composer's organ style. Written in 1959 it represents the composer at an advanced age, but still at the height of his compositional powers.

REFERENCES

Beckwith, John. "Healey Willan: The Man and His Music."
    The Canadian Forum, Vol. 52, No. 623 (December, 1972), pp. 32-34.

Bryant, Giles. *Healey Willan Catalogue.*
    Ottawa: National Library of Canada, 1972.

"Healey Willan." *Compositores de América/*
    Composers of the Americas, Vol. 6 (1960), pp. 111-116.

McCready, Louise G. "Healey Willan." *Canadian Portraits,*
    Toronto: Clarke, Irwin and Company Limited (1957), pp. 103-134.

Marwick, William E. "The Sacred Choral Music of Healey Willan." *Unpublished*
    Ph.D. Dissertation, Department of Music, Michigan State University, 1970.

Mercer, Ruby. "Healey Willan." *Opera Canada,*
    Vol. 9, No. 2 (May, 1968), pp. 16-17, 44.

Palk, Helen. "Canada's Greatest Composer." *The Book of Canadian Achievement,*
    Toronto: J.M. Dent and Sons Limited (1951), pp. 206-211.

Ridout, Godfrey. "Healey Willan." *The Canadian Music Journal,*
    Vol. 3, No. 3 (Spring, 1959), pp. 4-14.

Thistle, Lauretta. "The Healey Willan Exhibition." *The Canada Music Book/*
    Les Cahiers canadiens de musique, Vol. 4 (Spring-Summer, 1972), pp. 117-119.

Wyton, Alec. "Reminiscences: Healey Willan in a Conversation with Alec Wyton."
    Music: AGO-RCCO Magazine, Vol. 1 (December, 1967), pp. 24-27.

AN APOSTROPHE TO THE HEAVENLY HOSTS
1921
Healey Willan

Willan's anthem was commissioned by Dr. Fricker for performance by the Toronto Mendelssohn Choir in 1921. An urgent request by the publisher necessitated the completion of the work within three days—a deadline which the composer was able to meet. The greater part of the text is an adaption from the liturgy of the Eastern church; the music reflects the composer's style with a heavy leaning towards romanticism—particularly that of the Russian school.

The music commences very quietly, rising to ecstatic heights as the great figures of the Heavenly Hosts are invoked; semi-choirs add fervent *Amens*. The final section of the anthem is built on the German chorale *'Lasst uns erfreuen,'* with the composer's treatment resembling the polyphonic style of Bach in its highly contrapuntal *Alleluias*.

ANALYSIS:
The music requires a double chorus with a mystic semi-chorus adding occasional fragmentary utterances—almost antiphonally. The opening statement begins with the soprano and alto lines of the second chorus.

Example 1:

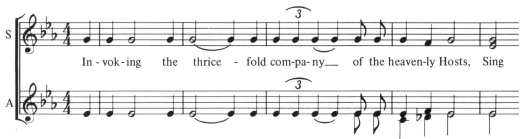

This chant-like introduction, although subdued in character, quickly builds dynamically at the words, 'Praise, O praise the King of Glory', and ends with the Mystic Choir chanting *Amen*.

Combining imitative contrapuntal lines with chordal progressions, the music continues with the words, 'Ye who perform the one Eternal Will . . .'

6

Example 2:

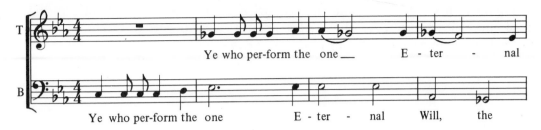

This short episode culminates in a repeated *Amen*.

The third verse unfolds in a smooth, undulating style at the words, 'Ye ministering Angels'.

Example 3:

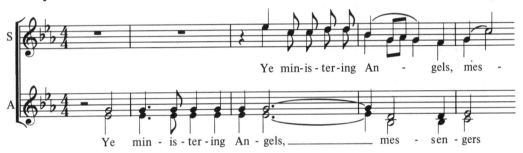

With antiphonal responses on the words 'Hail', the double choir unites in a hymn of praise, reaching a *fortissimo* climax at the words, 'Holy, Holy, Immortal'. Once more a mystic *Amen* concludes the statement. The final section of the work then follows with the chorus announcement of the German chorale, 'Ye Watchers and Ye Holy Ones' *(Lasst uns erfreuen)*.

Example 4:

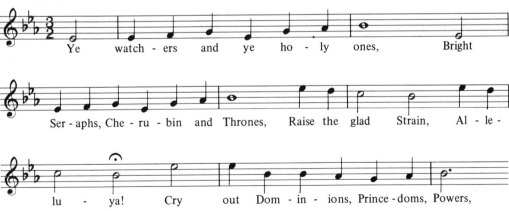

This fine melody provides a perfect expression for the composer's polyphonic and homophonic texture. Treated at first canonically, and then homophonically, the music majestically proclaims the *Alleluias* as it moves toward an exalting climax. Several more subdued repetitions of the *Alleluias* sung in chordal style preface the last two *Amens,* bringing the work to a very quiet, dignified, and satisfying close.

PIANOFORTE CONCERTO in C MINOR
1944
Healey Willan

The publication of Healey Willan's **Piano Concerto** in the year of his eightieth birthday was a most appropriate tribute to a man who laid a cornerstone of the art of serious composition in Canada. Through all his work he established himself as a composer who believed in tradition. This is no less true with the **Piano Concerto in C minor.** Udo Kasemets, in a discussion of the score observes that: "Even when he opens his concerto with a melody of wide romantic sweep, he keeps it balanced with a harmonic texture that is of classical clarity and strictly diatonic . . . Whenever dissonances are introduced in the harmony, they are justified by rigid part-leading and they never obscure the general direction of the progressions."

ANALYSIS:
The work is contained in one complete movement with three well-defined sections—*Allegro, Adagio, Con Spirito.* As is usual with music cast in a diatonic mold, there are frequent modulations to related major and minor keys. A two-measure drum roll precedes the piano soloist who enters with a six-measure theme in octaves.

Example 1:

The broad sweep of the opening theme is partially repeated; it reappears in simplified form against a quiet orchestral accompaniment.

Example 2:

With several successive phrases played by the soloist on material derived from the first theme, the tonality of the work is firmly established in C minor. Later on, the music modulates one semitone higher to C-sharp minor, with the piano still in octaves against a soft accompaniment. With several key changes and a thickening of the orchestral texture, the movement moves toward the *cadenza;* but not before a second theme in the related key of A-flat makes its appearance (2nd subject).

Example 3:

After the solo *cadenza*, one short orchestral *tutti* brings the music back into the tonic key with a theme obviously derived from the main subject.

Example 4:

Passing through a series of *arpeggio-like* figures, the music quietly modulates into the *Adagio*. Over a triplet figure in the piano, a solo theme for the English horn emerges in the key of B-flat minor.

Example 5:

Further development leads into the tonic major B-flat with the piano leading into a *quasi cadenza*. Passing through the key of D-flat major and E-flat major, the *Adagio* section concludes with a transition into C minor as the music moves into the final *con spirito*. At this point, a three-note pattern emerges which is later developed in other keys.

Example 6-a:

Example 6-b:

Short excursions into related keys with the solo line indulging in *arpeggio* and scale-like patterns propel the movement forward. As the music progresses there is a noticeable thickening of the orchestral texture. Finally, the three-note motif originally in C minor is recapitulated in the tonic major with a more majestic tempo. Marked *Nobilmente* in the score, the last few measures build toward the final climactic chords, bringing the work to a triumphant conclusion.

PASSACAGLIA and FUGUE No.2 in E MINOR
1959
Healey Willan

This work, written in the traditional style of the passacaglia and fugue form, was dedicated to Sir William McKie, former Organist and Master of the Choristers, Westminster Abbey. Although not of the proportions of his famous **Introduction, Passacaglia and Fugue,** the music is clearly stamped with the style that alone belongs to Willan. Closer acquaintance with the music — so typical of the composer's organ style — will well repay both organist and listener alike.

ANALYSIS:

A short introduction of eight measures precedes the ground bass on which the passacaglia is built. Here is the introduction.

Example 1:

Commencing moderately *forte,* the introduction reduces to a *pianissimo* at the cadence. At this point, the eight-measure theme which is in fact the ground bass, is heard in the pedals. It is a theme quite obviously in the key of E minor.

Example 2:

11

Traditionally, the form of the passacaglia was a slow dance in triple meter, constructed over a repeated ground bass. It became in effect, therefore, a series of variations built over a repetitive theme. In this work the same principle remains, with the ground bass appearing thirteen times — the original statement, and twelve variations composed either above or beneath this material.

A two-part strand of counterpoint is woven above the bass at the second entry of the ground bass.

Example 3:

Without any break in the flow of the music, the third and fourth variations continue with an added soprano line above the two-part counterpoint. The sustained tonic note in the top line is quite apparent at the commencement of variation three. The fifth entry appears in the top soprano line. Here it is quite obvious. More subtle however, is the bass entry one bar later in canon with the soprano line.

Between these two outside parts the alto and tenor lines move independently.

Example 4:

The sixth appearance of the ground occurs in the tenor line played by the left hand on the great organ. Below and above this theme independent lines weave melodic material. At the seventh entry the ground bass returns to the pedal organ. Here the music becomes more animated as the accompaniment is stated in triplets. This is particularly noticeable above the now familiar ground.

Example 5:

Entry eight continues in the pedals with the manual accompaniment gaining momentum through the use of sixteenth-note figures. This leads naturally into the ninth entry where the music becomes more brilliant. At this point the accompaniment consists of short three- and seven-note figures moving in parallel motion at the intervals of thirds and sixths (a traditional device).

Example 6:

Variation ten consists of descending *arpeggio-like* figures above the ground bass. Followed immediately by the eleventh appearance of the ground, the manual accompaniment is stated in an inverted order with the figures ascending. A more chordal texture then develops as the music broadens out and gradually moves toward an impressive climax on the dominant. After a momentary pause, the twelfth statement of the theme is played very softly in the treble line. Here the harmonies are very typical of the composer with their extensive use of chromaticism. This leads again to the final statement of the ground bass. Played quietly and expressively in the pedal line, the manual accompaniment modulates immediately into the related key of E major, where it remains to the concluding dominant chord.

The fugue subject is stated in the soprano line.

Example 7: *Subject*

Notice that the first two notes of the theme consist of the dominant proceeding to the tonic (b-e). At the fifth measure the *Answer* occurs in the alto line in inverted order (e-b). At measure nine the *Subject* is heard in the tenor line as the two earlier lines continue in the traditional manner with their countersubject material. The fourth entry *(Answer)* occurs naturally in the pedal part while the three independent lines weave their melodic strands above. With the exposition of both subject and answer stated, the composer continues with further development. Later, the *subject* is again stated. This time in the pedal line. Then free material *(Episode)* is introduced which is derived from earlier motivic ideas.

Example 8: *Episode*

It may be noticed that the composer's episodic material affords relief from the tonic key by the introduction of modulation. As any music student will know, this treatment is normal and quite traditional in the fugue form. In this fugue, Willan extends the middle section for thirty-two measures, developing the section with the usual devices of modulation, augmentation, diminution, and pedal point. Eighteen measures before the end, the *Subject* is again stated *fortissimo* in the pedal organ. Here there is a noticeable *allargando* as the tonal resources of the organ are called upon. One final entry in octaves in the top line adds strength and dignity to the work as it moves toward a grand *fortissimo* ending on the tonic major.

CLAUDE CHAMPAGNE
1891-1965
Composer and Teacher

"Claude Champagne is one of the first musicians in this country to be truly Canadian in the way that Tom Thomson and A. Y. Jackson are Canadian." These opening remarks were made by the Montreal critic Thomas Archer more than a decade ago in his introduction to a survey of the composer and his music. Today several years after his death, the late Dr. Champagne is respected as the man who "shaped a whole generation of French-Canadian composers" — a man whose musical influence through teaching and composing places him with Healey Willan in Ontario as one of the few outstanding 20th century musical pioneers in Canada.

Born in Montreal on May 27, 1891, Claude Champagne was raised in a family environment that encouraged his musical talent. His grandfather was highly regarded as a fiddler, and to his influence Champagne owes his early love and attraction for the modal flavour of Quebec folk music. At the age of ten he began piano studies. Later, he became the pupil of Roman Octave Pelletier, organist of St. James Cathedral, Montreal. While continuing his piano, he taught himself the violin, eventually receiving formal lessons from Albert Chamberland of Montreal.

In 1906 he graduated with the diploma of the Dominion College of Music, and in 1909 he graduated as laureate from the Montréal Conservatoire National de Musique. Champagne's mastery of instruments was later extended to include both the viola and saxophone. His first harmony lessons were given by Rodolphe Mathieu, allegedly a self-taught composer, but it was Alfred Laliberté who encouraged the young Claude Champagne to become a composer, to study compositional trends in Europe, and more particularly, to study with French teachers.

Recommended for further study in Europe, Champagne in 1921 secured a post in Paris as Dominion archivist. During his eight-year stay in France he came under the influence of André Gédalge, the teacher of such illustrious pupils as Maurice Ravel, Arthur Honegger, Darius Milhaud, and Joseph Bonnet. Continuing his composition studies with Gédalge until the latter's death in 1926, Champagne composed several early works, among them his **Suite canadienne** for choir and orchestra, completed in 1927. This work was received by Paris critics with considerable favour, gaining for the composer the International Folklore Award and the Beatty International Prize. It also became the first Canadian symphonic work to be performed by a major European orchestra.

On his return to Canada in December, 1929, Champagne became active in teaching and composing. In 1930 he accepted the post of teacher of harmony and counterpoint at the École de Musique d'Outremont, Montreal. He was also attached to the Montreal Catholic School Commission as co-ordinator of solfège in elementary schools. Champagne also taught at the Institut Pédagogique which became an important music centre for creative as well as executive art. Four years later he was invited by McGill University to teach baccalaureate classes at the McGill Conservatorium. It was during this time that Champagne began his 'truly remarkable courses in composition' which have since built up what Thomas Archer has no hesitation in calling the 'Champagne School.'

Throughout the 'thirties and 'forties Champagne worked increasingly in administrative positions. Teaching, editing, and organizing began to occupy more and more of his time — at the expense of his musical composition. Considering this aspect of his life, Archer observed: "Champagne is not a prolific composer. He is too great and honest a craftsman for that. His major works run into less than two dozen, but each in its own way is a masterpiece in its genre and likely to have lasting value in the future of creative art in Canada." Dr. Marvin Duchow of McGill University in a discussion of Claude Champagne's music reinforces this point: "The **Danse villageoise** — easily the most popular of all Canadian compositions — has withstood the cruel test of unceasing repetition retaining untarnished its aim of jaunty innocence throughout its innumerable performances in whichever of its several versions." Considering Champagne as a teacher, Duchow continued: "One of Champagne's distinctive gifts as a pedagogue was his extraordinary power of empathic insight, that is, his power to project imaginatively his own consciousness into the ideational world of each individual student. No less admirable was his ability and readiness to share with others his own profound sense of exhilaration in the musical experience as such."

From Champagne's catalogue of composed works several of the more significant are selected for discussion. Already mentioned is the **Danse villageoise** — *1930,* arranged in a number of different forms. Although the piece lasts only four minutes, the immense charm of the little work lies "not only in its recapturing of a vital phase of Canadian life, but also in its unpretentious simplicity and absolute truth to life." One version of the work is written for violin and piano, with two other versions for orchestra. **Images du Canada francais** for choir and orchestra — *1943,* is a large-scale musical tableau that evokes the atmosphere of old Canada; **Symphonie gaspésienne** — *1945,* published by BMI Canada was first performed in Montreal in 1947 and recorded by the CBC International Service; **Concerto in D** for piano and orchestra — *1948,* also recorded by CBCIS; **String Quartet** — *1951;* **Paysanna** for small orchestra — *1953,* first performed in Montreal in 1953 by a CBC Orchestra under Roland Leduc, and commissioned by the CBC to celebrate Queen Elizabeth II's coronation; **Altitude** — *1959,* for mixed choir, orchestra, and ondes Martenot, recorded by CBCIS on a Dominion Day record; and a miscellaneous number of vocal and instrumental compositions including arrangements of folk songs of French Canada.

As a conclusion to this brief biographical sketch of Claude Champagne there is a strong temptation to eulogize the man. However, perhaps one should be reminded of the many Canadian composers actively engaged in creative work as a result of his influence. Such composers as Violet Archer, Roger Matton, Clermont Pépin, Serge Garant, Gilles Tremblay, and Robert Turner — to name a few — received inspiration and musical guidance from Claude Champagne — Doctor of Music, *honoris causa.*

Considering Champagne's music as a whole, probably the most significant and representative of his mature works would include the **Symphonie gaspésienne, Concerto in D** for piano and medium orchestra, the **String Quartet,** and his last major work, **Altitude. Symphonie gaspésienne** — *1945,* has been called a musical travelogue utilizing melodies of the Gaspé region of eastern Quebec. Avoiding the literal quotation of authentic folk melodies, but still adhering to a conventional idiom, the composer has created in this work a tone poem of spacious proportions. "Unquestionably," says Marvin Duchow, "one of Champagne's most imposing creations, the **Symphonie gaspésienne** stands as a monument embodying his deeply felt vision of the physical and spiritual beauty of his native land." The work is particularly remarkable for its scoring, with the mysterious *pianissimo* opening; all that follows grows out of the bleak four-note motif taken up by the strings, chimes, and muted brass over the quietly throbbing rhythmic beat, muffled and austere. Describing the work Andrée Desautels says in *Aspects of Music in*

Canada: "The composer of **Symphonie gaspésienne** is certainly the greatest impressionist poet of our Canadian landscape."

Ten years have passed since the death of Claude Champagne. During this time a steadily growing realization of the composer's contribution to Canadian musical life has developed. The **String Quartet** and **Altitude,** recorded by the CBC, have been given further exposure, resulting in a greater awareness of the genuine originality of the music. The contemporary sonorities that are characteristic of these later works serve as a bridge to the present generation of younger composers living in Canada today. As with any composer, a carefully planned listening experience will help in furthering a deeper understanding and appreciation of his musical style. The descriptive analyses which follow may help in gaining enjoyment and further insight into one of the outstanding twentieth century Canadian musicians.

REFERENCES

Archer, Thomas. "Claude Champagne." *The Canadian Music Journal,*
    Vol. 2, No. 2 (Winter, 1968), pp. 3-10.

Bail-Milot, Louise. "Claude Champagne."
    Contemporary Canadian Composers
    (Keith MacMillan and John Beckwith, editors),
    Toronto: Oxford University Press (Canadian Branch), 1975.

Bail-Milot, Louise. "Les Oeuvres de Claude Champagne."
    Unpublished Thesis, University of Montreal, 1972.

"Claude Champagne." *Compositores de América/*
    Composers of the Americas, Vol. 6 (1960), pp. 42-46.

Colpoys, Andrew. "Claude Champagne, a Distinguished
    Canadian Composer." *Canadian Review of Music and Art,*
    Vol. 5, Nos. 6 & 7, (December-January, 1947), pp. 14, 28-29.

Duchow, Marvin. "Claude Champagne." *The Music Scene,*
    No. 243 (September-October, 1968). p. 7.

Duchow, Marvin. "Inventory List of the Compositions of Claude Champagne."
    CAUSM Journal, Vol. 2, No. 2 (Fall, 1972), pp. 67-82.

Walsh, Sister Ann. "The Life and Works
    of Claude Adonai Champagne." Unpublished Doctoral
    Dissertation, Catholic University of America, 1972.

SYMPHONIE GASPÉSIENNE
1945
Claude Champagne

This work is a tone poem of spacious proportions. It conjures up a mental picture of the austere Gaspésian landscape. Described earlier as a most significant example of Canadian impressionism, it has also been considered by Thomas Archer as 'one of the great artistic achievements of modern Canada'. This work is undoubtedly one of Champagne's most important compositions, and is a monument to the composer's artistic integrity. It is also one of the best known examples of orchestral tone-painting based upon a specific Canadian region.

ANALYSIS:
The work commences very slowly and very quietly in the low register of the strings. A continuously repeated note in the cellos and harp serves as a subdued accompaniment to the melodic line of the violas.

Example 1:

The introductory theme is announced by the violas beginning at the second measure.

Example 2:

After an ascending line, the theme quietly reverses its direction and continues downward. The persistent throbbing of the low strings creates a dramatically austere background for the percussive interjections of the vibraphone, harp and piano. Is this mysterious *pianissimo* opening suggestive of the bleak geographic region described — particularly the coastline? These opening measures are then repeated. Gradually the texture thickens as the pitch rises. Beginning with cellos and violas, and later with all the strings, another theme emerges.

21

Example 3:

A series of short woodwind melodies lead into an oboe solo which is accompanied by soft strings.

Example 4:

This nostalgic mood is preserved with the addition of flute and horns. Later in the score there is a slight quickening of the tempo as the clarinets and violins continue with the melody.

Example 5:

As the texture thickens to include all available instruments, there is a strong tendency toward lyricism with melodic elements dominating. Short fragmentary tunes in the brass may also be heard as well as delicate harp timbres. Without any break in the music, except a slight *allargando*, the tempo changes to *allegretto*. At this point, the time changes to compound quadruple, with the violins and oboes playing a new theme.

22

Example 6:

With a constantly changing texture, the music is propelled forward (dominated by the brass, and later by the woodwinds), until, with full orchestra, the sound intensifies as a climactic point is reached. Relief from this intensity comes with a return to earlier material. Here the flutes and violins play together.

Example 7:

A fast sixteenth-note passage leads to a *staccato-like* section dominated by the brass, which in turn subsides, making it possible to hear an English horn solo. Imitative treatment between strings and woodwinds creates a contrasting nostalgic mood once again, with the clarinet emerging as soloist.

Example 8:

Immediately the orchestral texture thickens and becomes more accented with a loud trumpet and trombone lead — but only momentarily — for there follows for the last time a more transparent and softer mood, which finally gives way to the full orchestra as it moves forward toward a grand *fortissimo* conclusion.

ALTITUDE
For Chorus and Orchestra
1959
Claude Champagne

In a review of a concert performance of **Altitude** Michael Olver in the *Montreal Star* wrote: ". . . It would be hard to find a more 'traditional' modernist than Champagne who died in December 1965, aged 74 and whose influence on the music of Quebec and of Canada is pervasive. **Altitude** was written in 1959 and is remarkable, among other things, for its use of the curious electronic instrument (curious in its own time, that is) called the ondes Martenot, a rather elementary and monophonic electronic organ played in a way that allows sliding up and down the scale. Besides using the ondes as part of his orchestral palette, Champagne brings his choir in with much the same purpose. Some of their words are in Huron Indian dialect, some a French translation of St. Francis of Assisi. But the intent of the choral singing is to add an extra dimension to the musical colour, rich and varied as it is throughout the tone poem's three parts . . ."

In this work the composer has drawn his inspiration from a Canadian landscape, presenting for chorus and orchestra his impressions of the Rocky Mountains. "The work is both descriptive and reflective: it evokes the rise and fall of mountain slopes and the mountain top atmosphere; it also looks spiritually inward and reflects on that communion with time and space which mountain-top sojourns so often arouse."

Champagne is explicit about his programmatic intentions. The score of **Altitude** is preceded by a topographical sketch which depicts the profile of the mountains. The various ascent, descent, summit and plateaus are linked with a number of emotions and thoughts which these contours and changes of scenery evoke in man, both primitive and modern.

Altitude is not merely a tone poem depicting the Canadian Rockies. It is a poem concerned with man's relationship with nature and its creator. The score calls for a mixed chorus in two passages, one a Huron prayer, and the other a text from St. Francis of Assisi. Divided into two sections subtitled 'Époque primitive' and 'Époque moderne', there is an orchestral meditation which forms a link passage between the two parts. In a short summary of the score, John Beckwith comments: "On the whole, this is a skilled work and one which is attractive to hear and which makes a strong and independent artistic impression."

ANALYSIS:

The introductory theme of 'Époque primitive' is announced slowly and very quietly by the cellos.

Example 1:

Commencing at measure twelve, *La montagne* (the mountain) is depicted in sound by rising seventh and ninth intervals in the strings.

Example 2:

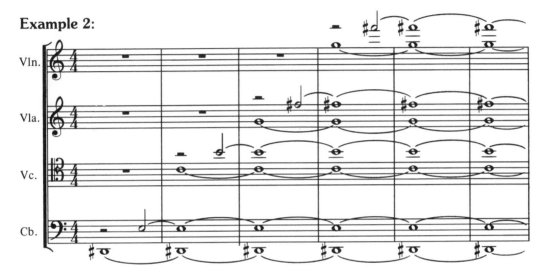

A repetitive sixteenth-note figure for two clarinets accompanies the quietly sustained chords.

This is immediately repeated for the second mountain in the profile, but sustained at considerable length. The addition of the ondes and the piccolo adds measurably to the colour. Ascending motivic elements in the woodwinds and strings depict the mystery of the mountains.

The rising tension in the music is like a description of the ascent towards the summit. At this point, a choral recitative in the language of the Huron Indians is introduced to symbolize man's act of worship.

Example 3:

Ta - la, Ta - la   A_____   ta - la ta - la

Harp and ondes join the gradual *crescendo*.

Example 4:

Soprano voices may then be heard singing four short eighth-note sounds on high B-flat.

This leads to a climactic point where the choir is introduced with the following rhythmic figure.

Example 5:

Using a Huron dialect, the unison choir creates an added dimension to the work.

Example 6:

26

Glissandos together with descending and ascending chromatic figures depict the avalanche and desolation. Unusual effects are also produced in the orchestral meditation where sustained chords in the strings accompany the ondes.

Example 7:

A short seven-measure phrase for the choir humming in harmony is followed by the ondes, which in turn leads into a unison passage for first and second violins.

The choir chanting on one note introduces the 'Époque moderne' section. A sustained chord in the strings accompanies the vocal line which rises gradually by thirds to a high A-sharp.

Example 8:

A second phrase, *Le feu*, is chanted on G accompanied by a *staccato* figure in the strings and a rapid undulating figure in the woodwinds. *La lune et les étoiles* commences later. The choir is then heard chanting in two parts accompanied by the ondes, celeste, and strings.

Example 9:

This leads into the *Coda*, which consists of the final twelve measures of the score. Here the vibraphone and harp, together with the full orchestra, depict once more the profile of the mountain, sketching in brief outline the mountain contours by a rising melodic figure. One final comment by the choir in four-part harmony brings the work to a conclusion.

STRING QUARTET
1951
Claude Champagne

The **String Quartet** was given its premiere performance by the Montreal String Quartet for the Montreal Pro Musica Society. In contrast to the previous programmatic music of Champagne, it is a work that is abstract in design, expressed in a highly dissonant idiom. Desautels describes the quartet as: ". . . a unique work pared down to essentials growing out of, and reflecting a solitude that seems to be the lot of the best of our poets and painters." Another of his previous students, Serge Garant, a Montreal composer, declares the work to be a 'model of contrapuntal writing', and compares the textures to those early Schoenberg works such as **Verklärte Nacht**. At the same time, he declares the melodic content has a certain airiness in common with, say the **Octet** of Milhaud!

Champagne's **Quartet** is undoubtedly a profound work, a reflection of the composer's mature musical and artistic development. Expertly balanced in the compositional elements of both sonata and fugue, the work occupies an important and unique position in Canadian musical literature.

ANALYSIS:
Movement I *Andantino*
The dissonant texture of this work is immediately obvious, beginning with the introductory measures. The first four measures are presented in open score for closer examination.

Example 1:

A noticeable increase in the tempo occurs shortly after the introductory statement. The first and second violin parts will illustrate.

Example 2:

With considerable independence in each instrumental line, the music passes through constantly changing time patterns, until a *pianissimo* section is reached *(subito)*. Here the first violin has an ascending and descending melody.

Example 3:

This short passage of thirty measures leads into the *Allegro moderato*. All four parts have rhythmic fluidity with noticeable triplet figures in each part.

Example 4:

With considerable tension generated by the rhythmic and harmonic elements, the movement gradually gains momentum ending on five loudly sustained chords.

Movement II *Andante*

The opening statement is given to two instruments — first violin and cello.

Example 5:

Commencing very softly, the violin line ascends in triple time while the cello line is in duple time. The second violin and viola join the ensemble at the thirteenth measure. Imitative lines between the first violin and cello lead to a solo cello part which is accompanied by sustained chords. This leads into a change in the time to compound duple. A repetitive five-note figure set against softly sustained chords is apparent at this point.

Example 6:

A characteristic ascending line may be heard in the cello part as the music alternates through a series of time changes between duple and triple. This tends to give the composition a fluid rhythmical element. Repetitive figures in the lower strings are also set against a rising line in the violin line as the work progresses. Later a rising line in the first violin imitates the opening statement.

Example 7:

Imitative entries in each of the remaining instruments are noticeable as the music moves toward the final few measures. A repetitive *spiccato* figure in the viola part is apparent at this point, assisting the movement as it builds toward the concluding sustained measures.

Sir ERNEST CAMPBELL MacMILLAN
1893-1973
Conductor, Organist, Teacher, Composer

A detailed chronological history of the 'highlights' in the life of the late Sir Ernest MacMillan looks very much indeed like a fairytale success story. Undoubtedly the young Ernest MacMillan was a child prodigy, but unlike many prodigies, was able to make the transition into adult professional life without dislocation of development. He was born in Mimico, Ontario, just outside Toronto. His father, Reverend Alexander MacMillan, was already well known as a hymnologist and in fact was later to become the principal editor of the United Church Hymnary, so the young MacMillan grew up in an environment of church music.

He took to the keyboard early, making a debut as organist in Toronto's Massey Hall at the age of ten, when his legs were still too short for his feet to reach the pedals. When the family moved to Edinburgh he continued his musical education there with Frederick Niecks and the blind organist Alfred Hollins. At the age of only 13 he became an Associate of the Royal College of Organists and three years later a Fellow (FRCO), winning the Lafontaine Prize for the highest mark of the year. During the same period he studied at

Oxford University, graduating with a Mus.B. degree in 1911. On the family's return to Canada he entered the University of Toronto as a student in Modern History.

In 1914 MacMillan sailed for France to further his musical studies. While he was on a short visit to Germany to attend the Bayreuth Festival, war broke out and the young musician was detained in Nürnberg and shortly after was interned until the war's end in the Ruhleben prison camp for British civilians on the outskirts of Berlin. During this period of confinement he wrote his **String Quartet in C minor** — Nürnberg, *September, 1914;* and **England, an Ode for Chorus and Orchestra** — *1918,* which he submitted to Oxford University (through the auspices of the Swiss Red Cross) as his thesis for his Doctor of Music degree. The degree was granted in the latter half of 1918 while he was still a prisoner. Prison camp life, frustrating as it was, nevertheless provided continuing opportunities for quiet study, and particularly for much practical experience in conducting and arranging music for the camp orchestra and operatic company.

The years following the war saw a whirlwind of activity. During 1919 he made a series of lecture-recital tours and was married (to Laura Elsie Keith) on New Year's Eve; in 1920 he was appointed organist and choirmaster of Timothy Eaton Memorial Church and to the faculty of the Canadian Academy of Music; in 1926, the year of his first annual performance of Bach's **St. Matthew Passion,** he was appointed Principal of the Toronto Conservatory of Music and the following year was appointed Dean of the Faculty of Music at the University of Toronto; in 1931 he conducted (with a broken right arm in a cast) the first concert of his quarter-century reign as conductor of the Toronto Symphony Orchestra.

In 1935 he was knighted by King George V "for services to music in Canada," the first musician outside Britain to be so honoured. During all this period and throughout the 30's he travelled extensively as lecturer, examiner, and adjudicator. From 1942-57 he was conductor of the Toronto Mendelssohn Choir; from 1949 until 1966 President of the Canadian Music Council; from 1947-69 President of CAPAC; from 1957-63 was a member of the fledgling Canada Council; from 1959-70 was President of the Canadian Music Centre; and from 1961-63 National President of Les Jeunesses Musicales du Canada.

His many honours and awards are too numerous to mention in detail here. He was granted honorary degrees by seven Canadian universities and by the University of Rochester, N.Y.; he was the first Canadian to be appointed Fellow of the Royal College of Music in London, England; in 1957 he was awarded the Richard Strauss Medal given by GEMA of Germany "in recognition of his outstanding services in protection of copyright;" was awarded the Canada Council Medal in 1964 and the following year the Award of Merit for the City of Toronto. In 1970 he was made Companion of the Order of Canada.

Obviously such a life must have been a busy one. But a creative artist must have time to think and it is understandable that most of Sir Ernest's output as a composer came in the early years, almost all before the 1930's. As Godfrey Ridout says in an article in *Music Across Canada,* August, 1963, "This side (composition) of his activities had been almost crowded out by the others. It seems now that, regardless of his skill and talent for composition, he apparently lacked the real drive and urge to continue in this direction." As Sir Ernest himself often said, "How can a conductor write his own music when his head is full of other people's!"

Even so, Sir Ernest has a creditable number of works either published or in manuscript. As well as **England** and the **Quartet** already mentioned, his **Two Sketches on French Canadian Airs** (for string quartet or for string orchestra) are well known, having been recorded several times; he arranged and edited two songbooks for schools; and arranged **Three Indian Songs from the West Coast,** and **Twenty-one Songs of French Canada,** for voice and piano; as well as **Six Bergerettes of Lower Canada,** for voices and chamber group; all these being evidence of his lifelong love of Canadian folk music and of the fruitful collaboration with his close friend, the late Marius Barbeau. On a larger scale he has also written a **Concert Overture** for the Toronto Symphony Orchestra; a **Te Deum,** for choir and orchestra; and **A Song of Deliverance** (at the close of World War II), also for choir and orchestra. Curiously, for a virtuoso organist (who once published an article entitled "The organ was my first love"), he wrote only one work for organ, the **Cortège Académique** and that not until 1953, for the occasion of the 100th anniversary of his alma mater, University College in Toronto.

Sir Ernest during his lifetime remained at the centre of Canadian musical life. His influence extended to such important organizations as the Canada Council, the Canadian Music Council, Jeunesses Musicales du Canada, and the Canadian College of Organists. At the high school and college levels many students belonged to the Sir Ernest MacMillan Fine Arts Clubs. Through radio and television appearances his musical influence grew. Although much has been written about Sir Ernest, there is little doubt that in the near future authoritative studies will be forthcoming that will more fully document the life and music of such a man. Fortunately we have several of his creative works on record. Listening to representative selections such as his **String Quartet** and **Two Sketches on French Canadian Airs** may give further musical insight.

REFERENCES

McCready, Louise G. "Sir Ernest Campbell MacMillan."
    Canadian Portraits, Toronto:
    Clarke, Irwin and Company Limited (1957), pp. 3-28.

MacKelcan, Fred R. "Sir Ernest MacMillan." *Queen's Quarterly,*
    Vol. 43, No. 4 (Winter, 1936-37), pp. 408-414.

MacMillan, Sir Ernest. "The Organ was my First Love."
    The Canadian Music Journal,
    Vol. 3, No. 3 (Spring, 1959), pp. 15-25.

Palk, Helen. "A Canadian Musical Knight."
    The Book of Canadian Achievement, Toronto:
    J. M. Dent and Sons Limited (1951), pp. 231-234.

Ridout, Godfrey. "Sir Ernest MacMillan: An Appraisal."
    The Canadian Music Educator, Vol. 6, No. 1
    (November-December, 1964), pp. 39-48.

Ridout, Godfrey. "Sir Ernest MacMillan: A Considered Appraisal."
    The Canadian Composer/Le Compositeur Canadien,
    No. 82 (July, 1973), pp. 6-14.

"Sir Ernest MacMillan." *Compositores de América/*
    Composers of the Americas, Vol. 11 (1965), pp. 75-82.

"Sir Ernest MacMillan." *Special Edition of The Canadian*
    Composer/Le Compositeur Canadien, No. 82 (July, 1973).

"Sir Ernest MacMillan . . . A Chronological History."
    Music Across Canada, Vol. 1, No. 6 (July-August, 1963), pp. 16-23.

STRING QUARTET in C MINOR
1914 *(revised 1921)*
Sir Ernest MacMillan

This work is the earliest example of Canadian music included in this series. Along with the composer's **Ode — England,** the first three movements were written during the years of the first World War; the last movement was completed on the composer's return to Toronto. A recording by the Amadeus Quartet gives a very fine reading of the work.

ANALYSIS:

Movement I *Allegro ma non troppo*

The introductory statement is played by the first violin, commencing on the dominant as follows:

Example 1:

Written in a lyrical flowing style, the impression is one of melodic interest. This emphasis is preserved throughout each of the subsequent statements of theme 1 — by the second violin, the viola, and the cello entries.

Example 2:

A secondary theme appears later, played in the top line, over a pedal-tone on the relative major E-flat.

Example 3:

With several modulatory passages, the music passes through development in both flat and sharp keys leading to a restatement of the exposition. The first theme is played by the viola at this point.

Example 4:

The second theme appears in the recapitulation a minor third lower.

Example 5:

A short *accelerando* leads the delightfully expressive movement to a close with a brief glimpse of the theme in the last few measures.

Movement II *Scherzo-Allegro Vivace*
This is a movement characteristically playful and dance-like written in triple time. The music opens softly with an ascending triadic figure built on the tonic minor chord.

Example 6:

Moving at a fast tempo, the figurations tend to move upwards in a light *staccato* style together with *pizzicato* chords.

Two motifs which have structural importance are also worth noting. The first is rhythmically centered and is built on the pattern ♪♪♪♪|♩ ♩ ♩. This may be heard several times in the movement. The second theme is a three-measure phrase announced by the viola against a *pizzicato* accompaniment.

Example 7:

Recapitulation of these basic themes occurs as the music rapidly moves toward the concluding two *pizzicato* chords. Altogether this is a movement that is appealing for its clarity and brightness.

Movement III *Lento ma non troppo*
This is a movement characteristically expressive, beginning in the relative major key of E-flat, with a flowing lyricism that creates a mood of peace and tranquility. The first theme which is predominant throughout is stated initially by the viola, with the second violin and cello parts accompanying the melody.

Example 8:

The viola then repeats and develops the theme in the subdominant.

Example 9:

Development of the opening three notes occurs both tonally and rhythmically. An example could be cited in the cello part where the rhythmic element is changed slightly.

Example 10:

After a modulation to the key of A major a secondary theme emerges played on cello. This short two-measure material will be heard also in other contexts.

Example 11:

In a short development of this material, together with a quickening of the pace and the use of sixteenth notes, the music provides a contrasting mood before the return to the original key and the first tempo. At this point, the first violin states the theme of the recapitulation. Short excursions through various keys lead the music quietly onwards toward the last few measures which end *pianissimo*.

Movement IV *Un poco lento—Allegro con fuoco*
Here is a movement of contrasting styles and tempi. A slow 36 measure section prefaces a bright snappy passage which in turn gives way to other alternate moods. Notice the changing meters, the key signature, and the ascending direction of the introductory statement.

Example 12: *Un poco lento*

Three measures — almost an extended cadence — played slowly and softly, are the prelude to the *Allegro con fuoco* section, whose first few unison measures bring a welcome relief to the previous sombre passage.

Example 13: *Allegro con fuoco*

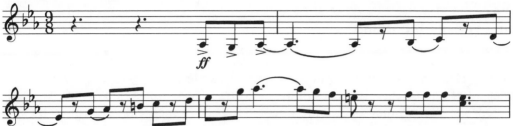

Here the *pizzicato* and the ascending lines give the passage an air of optimism and lightness. Later there is a return to the original tempo as the first violin announces another lyrical theme in E-flat major, built in an ascending direction also.

Example 14:

The rhythm of this theme is heard as a unifying element as the short passage progresses.

Contrast is again presented as the music moves into a faster passage once more. Here the viola may be heard with the ascending theme.

Example 15:

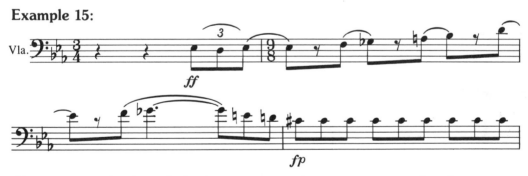

Changes in style through both *pizzicato* and *arco* treatment give the passage added colour. One further return to the lyrical material in the key of C major (the related tonic major of the work) gives contrast and variety of tonal resources. With a slight *accelerando* towards the last few measures, the music reaches a climax, bringing the four movements of the quartet to a very satisfying and rewarding conclusion.

TWO SKETCHES for STRING QUARTET
1927
Sir Ernest MacMillan

This work, based on two French Canadian folk songs, was originally written for the Hart House String Quartet. Today however, it is generally heard in a fuller version played by a string orchestra. The tunes upon which the sketches are based may be found in *Folk Songs of French Canada* edited by C. Marius Barbeau and Edward Sapir (Yale University Press, 1925). The first sketch, "Notre Seigneur en Pauvre" (Our Lord in Beggar's Guise), is a favourite topic of balladry in practically all Christian countries and exists in several versions. The melody recorded by Barbeau is as follows:

Example 1:

Saint Malo, the Breton port from which so many of the early settlers in Canada, beginning with Jacques Cartier, originally set sail, figures largely in French Canadian folklore. The present tune is described by Sir Ernest as "a great favourite and while not highly distinctive, it is characterized by a briskness and gaiety which commend it to the hearer." As is usual with many folk airs, there are many variants to be found. Probably the best known version is found in Gagnon's collection which differs slightly from the present version.

Example 2:

ANALYSIS:

The first sketch, although quite short, presents a mood of tranquility and meditation. The flowing contrapuntal lines, together with each of the several short phrases that rest momentarily at each cadence, probably contribute to the sense of calm and peacefulness that characterizes the movement. The opening phrase is played by the cello.

Example 3:

Imitative entries may be heard in each of the remaining parts. Commencing at the third entry, the theme is heard in the first violin.

Example 4:

Although the first sketch contains only seventy-seven measures, a strong sense of modality is maintained, preserving the music's authentic folk flavour. At the mid-point two short phrases leading from F-sharp minor to a restful E major give a subtle change in colour. This is followed by a return to the original mode bringing the movement to a sensitive close.

A Saint Malo: Here we have a complete contrast in mood with bright spirited music that is repetitious and joyful. A seven-note phrase commencing on the last beat of the measure introduces the music.

This is repeated in unison.

Example 5:

After twelve repetitions of the opening motif, the first violin announces the main theme which imparts a characteristic rhythmic pattern to the movement.

Example 6:

Against a pattern of *staccato* sixteenth-note figurations the theme is heard one octave higher.

Example 7:

Short excursions through various keys provide harmonic interest as the music pulsates ahead. In turn, each of the four parts claims attention as fragments of the theme are tossed to them — first the violins, then the cello, and finally the viola. Several measures before the end the first violin again repeats the thematic material against rising and falling scale passages, which in turn give way to the final *staccato* chords.

44

CONCERT OVERTURE
1924
Sir Ernest MacMillan

This work is scored for the usual orchestral forces including the harp. It commences slowly and softly with a drum roll which serves as an introduction to the opening cello statement. This theme consists of a two-measure phrase which is repeated by the cellos and then played by individual woodwinds and brass.

Example 1:

After a short introduction, the solo oboe announces a motif which is quickly transferred to other instruments. The rhythm is particularly noticeable.

Example 2:

Gradually the orchestral forces gather strength as the trombones ascend chromatically and the tempo accelerates. *Arpeggio* figures in the harp and glockenspiel also add colour toward the climax. A short pause precedes the *Allegro* which is announced by the trumpets.

Example 3:

Strings and woodwinds take over the theme and develop the material as the tempo broadens. Later modulatory development leads into an expressive melody. Here violas and cellos (with clarinet and English horn) play the new theme, which anticipates a gradual *crescendo* and rapid climax.

Example 4:

This is followed by a four-note solo on the horn and echoed on clarinet. From these few quiet measures there emerges a solo for harp and clarinet playing in unison over soft brass. The melody is a variant on the trumpet theme (illustrated earlier as Example 3).

Example 5:

This theme is then heard briefly in the strings and on flute and oboe. Again the orchestral texture thickens with harp and xylophone parts joining as accompaniment to the trumpet solo. Here the melody may be heard above the remaining orchestral forces.

Example 6:

Later a string quartet plays a chordal progression. Above this texture short woodwind solo passages may be heard — first the oboe, followed by flute,

46

clarinet, and flute again — all based on material previously heard. Then the volume rises to a *fortissimo* as the strings add weight to the reiteration. Short solo passages in the woodwinds follow, over quietly playing strings — but only momentarily, for again the texture thickens and broadens out as the basic pulse (which to this point has been the quarter) changes to a half note.

Only a few measures now remain in the score. Strong unison passages in the strings and a return to the original key of A major are noticeable as the music gathers momentum and, accompanied by *glissandos* on the harp with additional percussion effects, concludes on the tonic major chord.

MURRAY ADASKIN
1906
Violinist, Composer, Teacher

"There are three Murray Adaskins. One is a composer distinguished by melodic gift, pure form and symmetry; one is a professor whose prime interest in life is his students; the third is a man whose warmth, deeply-rooted humanity and uninhibited *joie de vivre* are a source of delight and strength to his friends." These words, written by Richard Savage in the September 1966 edition of *The Canadian Composer,* introduce us to the life and work of this distinguished Canadian musician.

Born in Toronto on March 28, 1906, Adaskin commenced his violin studies under the guidance of his elder brother Harry. More advanced studies were continued at the Royal Conservatory of Music, Toronto. Kathleen Parlow in New York and Marcel Chailley in Paris were also two of his influential violin teachers who helped and guided his musical studies as a young man. Later, after a number of years as a successful violinist, Adaskin turned his attention to composition. Among his teachers were the well-known Canadian composer John Weinzweig of Toronto, Charles Jones of New York City, and the world renowned Darius Milhaud of the Aspen School of Music, Colorado, U.S.A.

Adaskin's career spans almost half a century of playing, conducting, and composing music. From the early 1920's when he played violin in theatres and symphony orchestras, to his later years as teacher and professor of music at the University of Saskatchewan, he has continually devoted his time and energy to furthering and encouraging musical growth in Canada. His musical career is impressive. He played violin in the Toronto Symphony Orchestra as a young man (1926-36), he was violinist and director of music at the Banff Springs Hotel, Alberta, in the summer months, and also participated in many CBC radio engagements throughout this period.

In 1952, Adaskin was appointed to the faculty at the University of Saskatchewan, Saskatoon, remaining head of the music department until 1966. He conducted the Saskatoon Symphony Orchestra from 1957 to 1960, and later, in 1966, he became Canada's first Composer-in-Residence at the University of Saskatchewan — a position he held until his university retirement in 1973. Throughout these years, Professor Adaskin frequently appeared as guest-conductor with other orchestras in Canada, including the Toronto CBC Symphony, conducting his own compositions and the works of other major composers.

The years spent as a professor of music at Saskatoon were years in which Murray Adaskin became an established and recognized Canadian composer. His catalogue of works written and performed is impressive, with many pieces composed as a direct result of commissions from a wide variety of sources. Such works as his **Coronation Overture**—*1953;* **Rondino for Nine Instruments**—*1961;* **Grant Warden of the Plains**—*1967* (an historical opera set in the Red River Valley in 1826); and **Of Man and the Universe**—*1967* were each in turn commissioned by the CBC. Other works such as his **Saskatchewan Legend**—*1959;* **Concerto for Bassoon and Orchestra**—*1960;* **Divertimento No. 3**—*1965;* and **The Prairie Lily**—*1967* were commissioned by either individuals or organizations in Canada.

Among contemporary Canadian composers, there appears to be a lack of consensus on the nature and significance of the term 'Canadian music'. Is there such a genre? Do any of our composers consciously strive to create Canadian music? Murray Adaskin has lived in Canada all his life, and during that time he has absorbed perhaps consciously and unconsciously something of the spaciousness and vastness of the country. He and his wife have spent many summers at their cottage in Algonquin Park, Northern Ontario, and in the isolation of this area the composer has composed much of his work. Wynne Plumptre, who knows him well in the Algonquin Lake setting, describes this other dimension: "Murray loves the wild, he loves the water, he loves the trees, he loves the birds, he loves the wildlife, he becomes very much a part of Northern Canada, our 'cottage' country as we now call it." Perhaps this is the reason his music reflects the magic and spirit of that region.

Adaskin has succeeded in expressing in his music some of the special sounds of Canada, and many of his compositions have been affectionately coloured with folk-lore elements of Canada's early settlers, or, as in his popular **Algonquin Symphony,** evocations of Canadian Indian melodies and the calls and sounds of our wild-life. In a CBC commentary on Adaskin's **Algonquin Symphony,** Leonard Isaacs said: ". . . the texture is rather spare, the lines of the music are clear and clean, and the interstices are devoid of lush undergrowth. There is a feeling of great space and distance — not lacking in some asperity. Just as Aaron Copland's music is very American, so is Murray Adaskin's **Symphony** in some true and intangible way, very Canadian."

Living and working in Saskatoon for twenty years gave Murray and Frances Ada-skin opportunities to make many friends and to gain the love and respect of those who knew them. In a special CBC Radio tribute to the composer, entitled **Portrait of an Artist,** a number of musicians and close associates commented on his music. Speaking of Professor Adaskin, the U.S. composer Charles Jones said, "When you are a violinist, there is a certain inherent lyricism in what you are going to do; actually, the music comes from the fact that the violin really imitates the voice quite largely, and this usually brings about a particular kind of composer. I think this lyricism is everywhere in Murray's music." Eric Wild, conductor of the CBC Winnipeg Orchestra, also commented on Adaskin and his music: "I am especially fortunate as a conductor to have been able to perform most of his orchestral com-positions, and this has always been a joy and a pleasure and will continue to be so. There is no doubt in my mind that Murray has written great music." Victor Feld-brill also adds his assessment of Murray as a composer and of his attitude toward his art: "Adaskin has a fantastic spirit, tremendously encouraged all the time — I think he is one of the most optimistic people I have met — he loves to write — he loves to hear performances of his works, of course, and is one of the most enthu-siastic people I have ever encountered. Murray himself is a very fine craftsman and pretty well knows that things will come off in his orchestral scores. There are very few changes that have to be made after they are written."

Victor Feldbrill has this observation about the Adaskins living in the middle of the Canadian West. Why is he there? Why does he like it there? There are many rea-sons, including perhaps: "He has been given the kind of recognition in Saskatoon that very few composers get in other centres. He is respected there; I believe he was the first Composer-in-Residence at a university in Canada. This took a lot of administrative work away from him, which I am sure he preferred not to do, and gave him more time to think about his composing and just spending time with his students — living in Saskatoon gave him the opportunity to devote his time to the things he likes to do."

In 1969, Adaskin was the recipient of the Saskatoon citizen-of-the-year CFQC-TV award for his valued contributions to the cultural life of that city, as conductor, teacher, composer, and musician. In the summer of the same year, his new composition based on Eskimo themes (Qalala and Nilaula of the North), was premiered by the CBC, and in October of 1969, Canada's new National Arts Centre Orchestra performed his **Diversion for Orchestra** — *An Entertainment,* commissioned by the Arts Centre especially for the inaugural concert. It was the only work by a Canadian composer on the programme. Also that year, Adaskin's ten-year dream of having a resident string quartet at the University of Saskatchewan became a reality in the form of the Amati Quartet. Two further awards have recently been conferred upon Murray Adaskin. In 1970, the University of Lethbridge conferred an Honorary LL.D. degree, and in 1972, Brandon University conferred an Honorary Doctor of Music degree. Both honours signify in some measure the respect and esteem with which he is held in Canada.

Early in 1973, Murray and his wife Frances moved to Victoria, British Columbia, to enjoy their retirement years. However, these have not been years of idleness. On the contrary, the new life-style has created opportunities for teaching and for the creation of exciting new works. Among these are **Essay for Strings**—*1972;* and **Adagio for Cello and Piano**—*1973,* a work originally commissioned by the Victoria Conservatory of Music. Already this work has been performed in Los Angeles and Calgary by Talmon Herz of the University of Calgary. **Two Portraits**—*1973* (for violin and piano); and the **Quintet for Woodwinds**—*1974,* were also composed in Victoria. This latter work was commissioned by the University of Victoria's Pacific Wind Quintet through a Canada Council grant and has been played several times by the Victoria group. **Adagio**—*1974,* (for violin and piano); and **Nootka Ritual**—*1974,* are two of the composer's more recent works. **Nootka Ritual** was especially commissioned and performed by the Nanaimo Symphony Orchestra to celebrate the twenty-fifth anniversary of their organization. It has since been performed by the Toronto CBC Symphony Orchestra under the baton of Laszlo Gati, the conductor of Victoria's Symphony Orchestra. The **Adagio** is more correctly titled **T'Filat Shalom,** meaning a "Prayer for Peace." This work was commissioned by the Zionist Organization of Canada, and was premiered at the 41st National Convention in Jerusalem in February, 1975. The performance was particularly significant to Murray, for the violinist on this occasion was a young man named Jeffrey Krolik, a student of the composer. Jeffrey was a former pupil in Saskatchewan, and for his final grade-twelve year he moved to Victoria to study with the composer and complete his final year at Oak Bay Senior Secondary School.

These new compositions written by Dr. Adaskin reflect the strong neo-classic influence that has permeated his style since the days of his earliest works. Living as he does in the beautiful Uplands area of Victoria, he is able to respond to the beauty of nature that surrounds him. He works with a sense of serenity and purpose; in fact, the essence of his whole approach to life is to create and live in an environment where personal growth and development are continually enriched. When one converses with Murray, there is a realization that here is a person who is truly human, and one who cherishes the opportunity to give his best. Here is a composer who believes deeply in the worth of excellence.

Whether Dr. Murray Adaskin's works are created as a result of commissions or as expressions of his own individual creativity, his music may be frequently heard either on records, on radio broadcasts, or at live concert performances. As with most contemporary music, the listener is required to pay close attention if the listening experience is to result in greater understanding and deeper enjoyment. The three works selected for guided listening may assist in meeting this goal.

REFERENCES

Brandhagen, William L. "Asking Adaskin." *The Performing Arts in Canada,*
    Vol. 2, No. 2 (Spring, 1963), pp. 31-33.

"Murray Adaskin." *Compositores de América/Composers of the Americas,*
    Vol. 8 (1962), pp. 7-11.

"Murray Adaskin — A Portrait." *Musicanada,* No. 1 (May, 1967), pp. 8-9.

"Murray Adaskin: Composer in Residence." *Opera Canada,*
    Vol. 8, No. 3 (September, 1967), p. 22.

Savage, Richard. "Murray Adaskin: Composer, Professor, Gentleman."
    The Canadian Composer/Le Compositeur Canadien,
    No. 10 (September, 1966), pp. 4, 44.

SONATA for VIOLIN and PIANO
1946
Murray Adaskin

The **Sonata for Violin and Piano** was written during the period when Murray Adaskin was studying composition with John Weinzweig. It was first performed by the composer with his pianist-friend, Louis Crerar, to whom the **Sonata** is dedicated. The work has recently been recorded and released by the CBC in a new reading by the two distinguished recitalists in Toronto, Lorand Fenyves — violin, and Pierre Souvairan — piano. Although the **Sonata** is one of Adaskin's earlier works, it deserves attention, for it is extremely lyrical and tightly written. There is a 'leanness' to the piano part-writing that one associates with neo-classic influence, and the work also provides a useful comparison with later compositions written when the composer's artistic maturity was more fully developed.

ANALYSIS:

The *Sonata* is cast in three movements — *Moderato, Andante,* and *Rondo Allegro.* The influence of John Weinzweig is readily discernible, in that the composer has chosen to use twelve-tone techniques in the work. This is particularly true of the first movement where one is struck by the sheer lyricism of the music, obtained no doubt through the composer's understanding of the violin's ability to 'sing.'

Movement I *Moderato*

The tone row which is used freely throughout the movement is as follows:

Example 1:

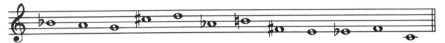

Twelve measures of three-part writing for piano serve as an introduction to the movement and lead into the opening statement for the violin. Several measures of the solo violin are presented below with the piano accompaniment. Notice the recurring two-measure *ostinato* figure in the piano line.

Example 2:

The composer's tendency to unfold the row gradually is noticeable in the second example. It takes the entire twenty-five-measure statement before all twelve tones of the row are announced. A short bridge passage for piano then leads into the middle section which is contrastingly faster. Here the violin and piano parts emphasize the major and minor second intervals that characterize the tone row.

Example 3:

In the following passage, one may notice the development of the five-note *ostinato* figure (see Example 2) which first occurred in the bass line of the piano part. A reappearance of this theme occurs with the figure played by the violin.

Example 4:

A return to the quieter mood of the opening completes the three-part form. With a reversal of the lines, both instruments bring the movement to a quiet close.

Movement II *Andante*

This short, peaceful movement is also ternary in design. The melodic and harmonic material is derived from this row.

Example 5:

The opening five measures for piano include the first nine tones of the row.

Example 6:

The violin entry at the sixth measure also emphasizes these tones melodically in its opening statement.

Example 7:

Adaskin's tendency to develop cells within the row is also noticeable at this point. In the second entry of the violin, the 10th, 11th, and 12th tones of the row appear. This is particularly evident in the middle section (B) where the tempo increases slightly. A four-measure excerpt from B illustrates this device.

Example 8:

A new rhythmic figure on piano creates more movement in this middle section, as the music grows in intensity. A return to the opening statement (recapitulation) signals the former peaceful mood. Here the music is transposed a fifth higher.

Example 9:

A few further measures, sustained and peaceful in character, bring this second movement to its conclusion.

Movement III *Rondo Allegro*

This lively movement commences with a repetitive seven-note figure on the piano. As an *ostinato,* it serves to propel the music ahead.

Example 10:

Twelve measures on piano serve as an introduction to the solo violin which introduces section A with this vigorous statement.

Example 11:

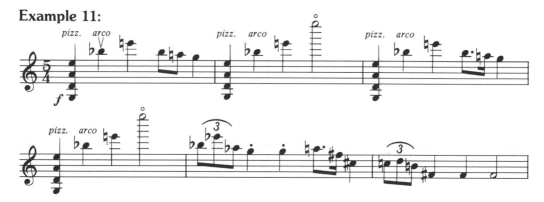

With imitative phrases, the music develops section A of the rondo in $\frac{5}{4}$ meter, and then quickly leads into the B section (in triple meter), beginning softly. Four measures will illustrate this contrasting section.

Example 12:

A return to the violin theme, as shown in Example 11, brings further development of the rondo. A slight *diminuendo* and *rallentando* preface the C section. Here is the muted violin entry in duple meter.

Example 13:

Notice both the imitative phrases between instruments and the two-part dialogue that develops. Two measures of solo piano prepare for the return to section A in the original $\frac{5}{4}$ meter. In this final appearance of the seven-note theme (see Example 10), the piano part is written in octaves. Further development of both piano and violin thematic patterns urge the music towards a climactic point, and with one final flourish it reaches an exciting conclusion.

DIVERTIMENTO No.3
1960
John Weinzweig

This third composition in the Divertimento series was especially commissioned by the Saskatoon Symphony Orchestra. Written specifically for solo bassoon and strings, it has a "decided jazz outlook in its phrasing, structure, and rhythmic fluidity. It is organized in the serial technique with rhythmic figures favourable to the swing manner."

Because of the composer's unique treatment of the row, both melodic and harmonic elements develop in a stylistically consistent manner. Previous compositions utilized a different tone series for individual movements, but in this work one tone-row has been used throughout the entire work, resulting in music that is structurally unified, original in design and texturally transparent.

ANALYSIS:
Movement I *Moderate Swing*
The work is derived from a tone-row which offers several obvious tonal centres.

Example 1:

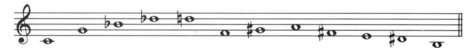

All melodic and harmonic elements are generated from this series of tones. By using various forms of the row — original , retrograde, inversion, and retrograde inversion, together with the many possible transformations obtained through transposition, the composer has demonstrated his compositional skill by producing an artistic work of considerable merit.

The first violins announce the introductory statement.

Example 2:

At the ninth measure the solo bassoon (accompanied by a *pizzicato* bass) makes its entry with a repeated four-note fragment (the first four tones of the row).

Example 3:

With three- and four-note cells, each section of the strings makes its appearance. A few measures later a four-note *staccato* figure in two- and three-parts accompanies the solo bassoon. A change in tempo is noticeable at the viola entry. Notice also how individual string lines add their commentary in the nature of dialogue.

Example 4:

Brief motivic elements on bassoon and in each of the string parts are encountered as the short first movement develops to its conclusion.

Movement II *Slow*

This lyrical movement commences with three measures in $\frac{5}{4}$ meter. The bassoon then enters with its theme at the fifth measure in $\frac{4}{4}$ meter. With repeated notes in each of the several phrases, the melody has a somewhat nostalgic character.

76

Example 5:

A short string interlude leads into an *ostinato* played *pizzicato* on double-bass.

Example 6:

Over this bass figure, the bassoon announces the second theme which is derived from the row by using the retrograde inversion form.

Example 7:

The development which follows reveals the composer's ability to write music that is derived from the row. With rhapsodic treatment in the solo part together with canonic treatment in the strings, the movement concludes on a quiet *pianissimo* note.

Movement III *Fast Swing*

The final movement is played at a brisk tempo. A rhythmical 17-measure introduction by the strings precedes the bassoon entry. Decidedly syncopated, the theme is presented as follows:

Example 8:

A three-note *staccato* figure dominates the accompaniment. The second bassoon entry emphasizes the syncopation.

Example 9:

With *pizzicato* and *staccato* treatments, the string accompaniment produces a variety of textures to accompany the first violin's theme. The swing element is developed further with the bassoon's third entry.

Example 10:

This leads into a change to duple meter. *Staccato, pizzicato,* and *spiccato* styles add colour to the texture as do the constantly-changing dynamics. A return to the original tempo then occurs as the first violins play. This is answered imitatively by the second violins and violas. Notice the change from quadruple meter to triple meter in Example 11.

Example 11:

The bassoon entry which follows is similar in design to the instrument's opening statement (third movement, Example 8).

Example 12:

Several more short thematic episodes by the solo bassoon together with fragmentary figures in the accompaniment propel the music onwards toward the last few measures, which conclude on a decisive four-note figure in the strings.

Compositions which feature solo bassoon with instrumental ensemble are not overly abundant in Canadian musical literature. Owing to such fine bassoonists as George Zukerman, this work is rapidly gaining a permanent place in the standard repertoire, and as a work of substance it is becoming recognized as a significant contribution to the available literature. Familiarity with the music should prove to be an enriching experience for performer and listener alike.

DIVERTIMENTO No.5
1961
John Weinzweig

Divertimento No. 5 for trumpet, trombone, and symphonic wind ensemble belongs to the series of six pieces in this form composed to date. The work was commissioned by the American Wind Symphony Orchestra for its Music and Arts Festival in Pittsburgh, Pennsylvania during the summer of 1961. Although the wind ensemble is a departure from the composer's Divertimenti set for solo woodwinds and strings, the basic plan is similar. As in the remainder of the series, the design is a modified three-movement concerto plan of fast — slow — fast.

As explained in the preface of the score published by Leeds Music (Canada) Limited, "for the greater part of the work, the trumpet and trombone soloists engage in duets based on contrapuntal rhythmic structures, usually without accompaniment; in the second and third movements they break off into solo playing with orchestral support." With a full battery of wind instruments and percussion, the scoring, although sparingly employed, provides a most satisfactory expression for the composer. As in all of Weinzweig's scores, the music develops as a direct result of his ability to utilize the row for his melodic and harmonic material.

ANALYSIS:
Movement I *Fast*
This first movement is written in the form of a rondo with the principal theme presented by the soloists and varied by inversion and retrograde in the repetitions. As in other works by Weinzweig, the tendency to manipulate various segments of the row, developing both melodic and harmonic material, is very apparent. A close inspection of the row will show the intervals produced between succeeding tones in the row, and the similarities obtained between the first six tones (hexachord) and the remaining six tones.

Example 1:

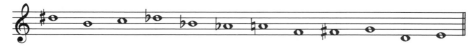

The introduction consists of a short rhythmic statement in the horns (a major 3rd apart) and woodwinds. This is the first presentation of the row, and it leads into the opening phrases played by the two soloists, trumpet and trombone, which complete the second presentation of the row in two-part counterpoint.

Example 2:

Examination of the first three solo measures in Example 2 will show how Weinzweig segments the row — a treatment or tendency on his part to expose the row in segments or cells. This 'unfolding' of the row is strongly characteristic of the composer and provides insight into his method of development. He also retraces certain tones. For example: In the first measure of Example 2, tones 1 — 6 are used. The third measure commences on the fourth tone of the row and uses tones 4 — 9. The fifth measure again retraces and uses tones 7 — 12. These are methods of 'working the row' that Weinzweig discovered for himself, and do not emulate the Viennese school of Schoenberg or Berg. To detail the many possible permutations of the row, although of interest to the analyst, would probably prove both time-consuming and onerous in the classroom. A presentation or description of the rhythmic and melodic development, together with the specific instrumentation will suffice as a guide through the listening experience.

The second statement on trumpet and trombone is again in the nature of a dialogue. This presentation utilizes the row transposed down a minor third beginning on C.

Example 3:

With interjections by the accompanying ensemble, the music progresses through a series of statements and counter-statements producing a light and, at times, comical mood. The rhythmic vitality and percussive interjectory nature of the movement exploits the two- and three-note cell construction for both soloists and accompaniment. At page 21 in the score, the two soloists imitate each other in dialogue form.

Example 4:

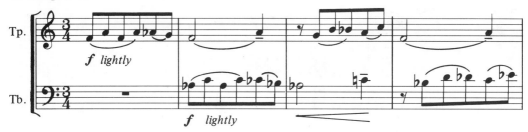

With a variety of dynamics, the movement reaches its conclusion, but not before the percussion have added their comments!

Movement II *Slowly, expressively*
The solo trombone and trumpet again introduce the movement. The tones are derived from the first hexachord transposed down to F and inverted. Both instruments are muted, and, in the form of a dialogue, create two-part counterpoint. The rhythm and dynamics are important elements in the announcement of the theme.

Example 5:

After a seven-measure statement, the oboes commence using tones derived from the tenth transposition of the row — only in retrograde form. (One must remember when demonstrating these thematic elements on the piano that the minor seconds on the piano have a sharper tension than they have on the wind instruments.) An interesting figure in the percussion follows. The composer describes it as an important break-through in his percussion thinking. The tom-tom, vibraphone, and glockenspiel form a trio, and later the timpani, tenor drum, suspended cymbal, and tom-tom provide a quartet accompaniment to the solo trumpet and trombone. Here is the trumpet part.

Example 6:

The unaccompanied duet commences once again. Trilling woodwinds then produce an unusual interjection and contrast, which leads again to the brass dialogue. The sustained character of the music and the unhurried tempo produce a mood of tranquility and one which creates a satisfying contrast between the two outer movements.

Movement III *Moderately fast*
The immediate impact of tuba and piccolo is one of comic relief — a humorous dialogue between a 'fat' sound and a very high 'thin' sound. The opening tuba line comes from the original row transposed from D-sharp down to C. Again, only the first hexachord is used. The piccolo answers with the same hexachord in inverted form. The contrasting voices coupled with a rhythmic vitality very reminiscent of jazz, create an overall mood of fun and excitement.

Example 7:

The first entry of the solo trombone begins at the thirteenth measure, using the tones of the row transposed to begin on G-sharp.

Example 8:

This phrase is immediately answered by the trumpet in the inverted form.

Example 9:

With passages for the soloists, both together and separately, the music progresses and develops at a fast pace. The emphatic rhythms and *staccato* patterns, together with a most energetic percussion section, all contribute to the playful mood that pervades the movement. The final re-appearance of tuba and piccolo accent even further the humour that underlies the entire work.

WOODWIND QUINTET
1964
John Weinzweig

The *Woodwind Quintet* is one of Weinzweig's most widely-performed works. Composed during 1963-64, it was dedicated to the late John Adaskin, a personal friend of the composer and former Executive Secretary of the Canadian Music Centre. The first performance was presented by Ten Centuries Concerts in Toronto on January 10, 1965, performed by the Toronto Woodwind Quintet. A recording of the work was released in 1967 by RCA Victor and the International Service of the CBC under the label *Music and Musicians of Canada,* Volume VI. The work is still obtainable from the CBC *Canadian Collection*. In a review of the music, Kurt Stone published the following comments in *The Musical Quarterly:* "His **Woodwind Quintet** has a well-shaped, spirited, even amusing first movement which represents a number of clearly outlined thematic ideas and then puts them through their paces. The second movement is more atmospheric and subjective in character, but it too, shows clarity of structure, economy, and considerable expressive originality and inventiveness. The last movement is as entertaining as the first, yet quite different in character. Weinzweig is a real composer."

ANALYSIS:
Movement I *Fast*
The first movement, in fact the entire work, is built from one tone row. Examination of this row will establish the pattern of minor third and minor second intervals that constitute each of the four three-note segments. All subsequent melodic and harmonic material is derived from this row or one of the possible permutations of the row.

Example 1:

The composition is scored for flute, oboe, clarinet, horn, and bassoon. The first presentation of the row splits the series into 8 tones and 4 tones. Tones 1 — 8 constitute a vertical harmonic presentation and can be seen in the first measure. Tones 9 — 12 are the melodic presentation and will be found in the third and fourth measures, played by the oboe.

Example 2:

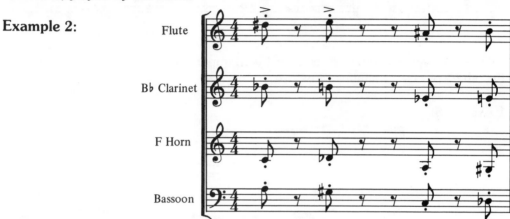

The second measure is a repeat of the first with a slight rhythmic change. Notice how the notes of each melodic line lie one semi-tone apart. This is an important element in the music, for the work has strong jazz connotations which derive from the characteristic semi-tone inflections found in jazz. The opening statement is as follows:

Example 3:

Played *staccato* at a brisk pace, the introductory harmonic material prefaces a short oboe motif. Here we discover, for the first time, tones 9 — 12 of the row.

Example 4:

This is followed a few measures later by an important bassoon entry consisting of two short phrases, imitative in nature.

Example 5:

Examination of this theme will demonstrate the two- and three-note cell construction and the derivation of the tones themselves from the first six tones of the row, transposed down from C to G and then inverted. Professor Weinzweig would label this I-6 because G is the sixth tone (inclusively) down from C and each of the tones is inverted from the original. Imitative phrases occur among the remaining instruments. An example may be heard in the clarinet part, emphasizing the dialogue that takes place between pairs of instruments.

Example 6:

Two remaining points of interest are: (a) motifs in the bassoon, oboe, and clarinet parts are repeated several times, and (b) in this movement, the horn has no solo line. With a combination of vertical and horizontal textures, the development leads quite logically to the last few measures which alternate dynamically between loud, soft, and very soft.

Movement II *Slow*

The opening motifs, played slowly, are given to the clarinet, flute, oboe, and bassoon in succession. It may be noticed that here we have the original row segmented into four cells. This segmentation of the row is a typical example of Weinzweig's habit of gradually unfolding the row.

Example 7:

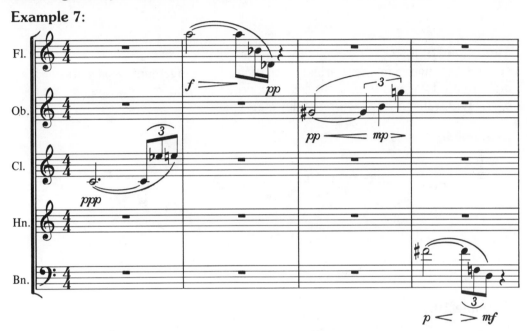

Again it may be noticed that the first measure consists of two intervals (a minor third and a minor second) which are in retrograde form in the second measure. It may also be interesting in class to speculate on measures three and four!

After a short introductory statement, a two-part accompaniment for clarinet and bassoon begins. This five-note figure has a rhythmic *ostinato* quality.

Example 8:

Joined by the solo horn, and later by the flute and oboe, the texture continually changes to produce a colourful instrumental palette, adding interest to the rhythmically charged movement.

Movement III *Fast*

A repetitive figure in the clarinet introduces this movement. Again the figure is built from a two- and three-note cell. The notes are derived from the first six tones of the row transposed down one full tone.

Example 9:

At the twelfth measure, the flute commences a motif that is an inversion of the opening intervals and contains tones 10 — 12 of the row.

Example 10:

With a noticeable thickening of the texture, a new accompanying figure is introduced in the flute and oboe.

Example 11:

This is an accompaniment figure for the horn which commences with a *glissando*.

Example 12:

Further entries occur in the oboe line, and a few measures later the flute follows with a new rhythmic figure of a repetitive nature.

Example 13:

This is quickly tossed to the clarinet imitatively. Further development of a three-note cell continues, as the music maintains its drive towards the last few measures. With considerable emphasis on irregular rhythms, the music moves logically toward its conclusion on a three-note figure, again emphasizing the germinal idea which is central to the form and character of the entire work.

This work has been discussed in some detail to further one's understanding of twelve-tone music as composed by Weinzweig. In a discussion with the composer he emphasized the importance of the row: "I don't make up a row at random; I decide first of all what style of music I am going to write, and I build and create that style through the arrangement — the selection of intervals. The row then guarantees me a unity of style." Several repetitions of the music with guided attentive listening should produce rewarding results.

TO THE LANDS OVER YONDER
1953
John Weinzweig

John Weinzweig has made free use of an authentic Coppermine Eskimo dance-song in his four-part setting for mixed chorus. The song is one of a collection gathered during the Canadian Expedition (1913-18) for the Canadian government under the leadership of Commander Vilhajalmur Stefansson. The music is an original conception based on a study of Eskimo folksongs and is set in a low key to emulate the native timbre insofar as possible. It is not a difficult work to sing and could provide an added opportunity for classroom participation.

TO THE LANDS OVER YONDER
(MIXED CHORUS—A CAPPELLA)

JOHN WEINZWEIG

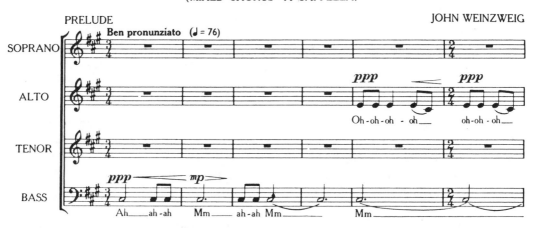

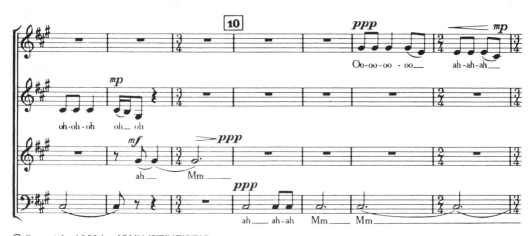

93

JEAN PAPINEAU-COUTURE
1916 –
Composer, Professor

Professor Jean Papineau-Couture of the University of Montreal's Faculty of Music is without doubt one of the musical leaders in Canada today. In the Province of Quebec, where he is very well known, he is held in the utmost respect as both teacher and composer. Unfortunately, many English-speaking Canadians have not been sufficiently exposed to the music of this composer, and as a result lack understanding of his influence on the musical scene. His music is, however, heard considerably more often over French-speaking radio stations in this country, and his name is gradually becoming more familiar in other parts of Canada.

Born in Montreal on November 12, 1916, Jean Papineau-Couture was raised in a musical environment. His mother, Marie-Anne, gave him his first piano lessons, and although he never knew his paternal grandfather, Guillaume Couture, the family influence of a man described as 'one of the great pioneers of music in Canada' must surely have been considerable. More advanced piano studies were continued with Françoise d'Amour and Léo-Pol Morin. Taking a *baccalauréat ès arts* at Jean de Brébeuf Collège in Montreal, he also studied harmony and counterpoint with Gabriel Cusson.

A grant from the Quebec Provincial Government enabled Jean to pursue studies in the United States. At the New England Conservatory of Music in Boston, he studied conducting with Francis Findlay. Graduating with a Bachelor of Music degree in 1941, he went in the following year to the Longy School in Cambridge, Mass., where he studied fugue, analysis, and composition with the famous French teacher, Nadia Boulanger. After a one-year study with Boulanger, Papineau-Couture returned to Montreal to teach. However, he later resumed studies with Miss Boulanger at Madison, Wisconsin, and again for another year at Montecito, near Santa Barbara, California. Discussing the influence of the illustrious Nadia Boulanger on Papineau-Couture, John Beckwith in the Winter 1959 issue of *The Canadian Music Journal* commented: "In Papineau-Couture she seems to have stimulated a high standard of personal drive and accomplishment . . . it seems clear that he gained under her guidance the contrapuntal and formal practice that makes him today technically one of the best-equipped composers in Canada."

Papineau-Couture's musical career is impressive. Commencing as a teacher of piano at Jean de Brébeuf Collège, he later was appointed professor at the Conservatory of Music in the Province of Quebec. In 1951, he was appointed professor in the Faculty of Music at the University of Montreal, and in 1968 he became dean of music. His professional leadership is evidenced in his associations with the Canadian Music Centre (board of directors and past president), the Canadian League of Composers (past president), the Canadian Music Council (past president), the Quebec Arts Council, the Académie de Musique du Québec, and the Société de Musique Contemporaine du Québec (founding president, 1966-73). In addition to his professional affiliations, Jean Papineau-Couture has, since his student days, been the recipient of a number of awards and scholarships. Most noted are: Orchestra Symphonique de Montreal prize for **Pièce concertante No. 3—1960;** an honorary LL.D. degree from the University of Saskatchewan in 1967, and the Canadian Medal of Service in 1968.

Before looking more closely at the music of Papineau-Couture, we may gain a deeper impression of his attitudes and musical style by reviewing one or two of the composer's own statements about himself and his music. Speaking of his early student days, Papineau-Couture said: "Modal style had a great influence on me because I had practised Gregorian accompaniment to a great extent, and this, added to my interest in Fauré's music, started my development along modal lines. From there I went on to a concept in which modal alternated with Debussy's whole-tone scale. I next decided to follow the neo-classic style with its possibilities in the field of bi-tonality and bi-modality, together with its capacities of a simultaneous chord in major third and minor third. I decided to explore the entire field of the neo-classic style but I kept few of the works I turned out in those days — except **Les Eglogues,** written on a poem by the late Pierre Baillaugeon. I feel it is interesting that I should have kept them because they show beyond any doubt that there was a development taking place at that time. The first one is impressionistic in style, the second definitely more so, and the third becomes something of the neo-classic line!"

Yolande Rivard, a Montreal freelance writer, discussing the composer's musical development in *The Music Scene,* quotes Papineau-Couture as saying: "Little by little, I came to give up tonality altogether, but I decided to keep my system of anchor points because I knew these points could very well become a kind of melodic design or, if you prefer, a rhythmic design, a contrast of orchestration, or of texture — it doesn't matter."

From the early tonal period of Papineau-Couture's music to the latest works, changes have come gradually and as a natural development. It is no secret that he has been influenced, as have many other contemporary composers, by the music and teachings of Stravinsky. In a discussion of Papineau-Coutures **Pièce concertante No. 1**—*1957,* for piano and strings, John Beckwith wrote in *The Canadian Music Journal:* "The work is formally a single large frontward-backward design. Examples of this type of musical architecture are found in Berg's **Lulu** and the recent **Canticum Sacrum** of Stravinsky, but Papineau-Couture's piece is larger than either." And of an earlier work entitled **Poème**—*1952,* Beckwith states: "The middle section has an allegretto theme suggestive of the balletic Stravinsky."

In the opinion of the composer, the principal works from the fifteen year period 1942-57 are the **Eglogues**—*1942,* particularly the third; the **Concerto Grosso**—*1943,* which incidentally was not premiered till fourteen years later in 1957; the **Aria pour violon seul**—*1946;* **Papotages**—*1949,* a large-scale ballet for full orchestra; the **Concerto pour violon et orchestre de chambre**—*1952;* and the **Psaume 150**—*1954.* The Psalm, written for soloists, choir, winds, brass, and organ, has been recorded by the CBC in Montreal under George Little's direction, and later performed by the Festival Singers of Canada.

Although one cannot easily divide Papineau-Couture's music into specific periods, from 1957 onwards there appears to be a noticeable change and turning-point in the composer's output. The **Pièce concertante No. 1** for piano and strings, subtitled *Repliement* (folding back), demonstrates a more radical departure from the earlier works. There is an increasing concern with intellectual order through the formal application of twelve-tone devices. The contrapuntal skill and the ability to solve structural problems inherent in the frontward-backward design is further evidence of the composer's mastery of musical form. Other works in the Concertante series that have received critical acclaim are: **Pièce concertante No. 4** for oboe and string orchestra—*1959,* premiered at the 50th anniversary of the University of Saskatoon; and **Pièce concertante No. 5** *(Miroirs)* for orchestra—*1963,* recorded on the Place des Arts souvenir record, especially commissioned for the inauguration of Salle Wilfred Pelletier, Place des Arts, Montreal.

In his latest works, Jean Papineau-Couture has shown an interest in tone colour which had not appeared in his important vocabulary since his earliest forgotten compositions. The first work he decided to keep had a trace of this tone colour, but it later disappeared completely from his music. However, starting with compositions like his **Concerto for Piano and Orchestra**—*1965;* **Viole d'amour**—*1966,* for mixed chorus; the **Sextuor**—*1967,* for instrumental ensemble; **Paysage**—*1968,* for choir and instrumental ensemble; **Oscillations**—*1969,* for orchestra; and **Nocturnes**—*1969,* for instrumental ensemble; there may be found a greater preoccupation with tone colour. Discussing this particular aspect of his compositions, Professor Papineau-Couture comments: "I have used orchestral mixtures which certainly do not belong to me exclusively, but they are orchestral mixtures which I had not previously used, and which I managed to handle in a manner that is exclusively mine."

Of the important works composed during the last ten years, certain pieces should be mentioned for their significance. **La Suite Lapitsky** — *1965,* was performed by the Montreal Symphony Orchestra on February 6th, 1973 under the baton of Franz-Paul Decker. Commenting on the event, Eric McLean of the *Montreal Star* wrote: "Decker has shown great perception in reviving it for one of the adult series where it deserved a hearing in the first place. It is energetic and clever music, designed for the conventional symphony orchestra, and couched in perfectly accessible language . . . Altogether the suite struck me as one of Papineau-Couture's most ingratiating works." Two recent works for solo voice also have particular interest. **Contraste**—*1970,* for solo voice and orchestra, was composed on a commission from the Montreal International Vocal Competition for the 1970 competition. **Chanson de Rahit**—*1972,* for soprano, clarinet, and piano, was given its world premiere performance on March 1, 1973 at the University of Montreal.

Much more could be said about Jean Papineau-Couture and his music. Any summary, however brief, should acknowledge the composer's distinctive contribution to Canadian music. Throughout his career he has explored several approaches to musical composition, always pursuing his investigation to the end, and never tiring in his quest for thoroughness and perfection. In many respects, like Stravinsky, he is a champion of pure music that is intellectually conceived, and devoid of emotion. It is obvious that the man is very much of his time, a mature craftsman who is skilled in the many compositional techniques he employs, and who as a composer and influential teacher is one of the foremost living Canadian composers.

REFERENCES

Beckwith, John. "Jean Papineau-Couture." *The Canadian Music Journal,*
    Vol. 3, No. 2 (Winter, 1959), pp. 4-20.

"Jean Papineau-Couture — A Portrait." *Musicanada,* No. 3 (July, 1967), pp. 8-9.

"Jean Papineau-Couture." *Compositores de América/Composers of the Americas,*
    Vol. 5 (1959), pp. 57-62.

"Jean Papineau-Couture." Brochure, BMI Canada Ltd., 1970.

Poulin, Roch. "L'oeuvre vocale de Jean Papineau-Couture."
    Unpublished Thesis, University of Montreal, 1961.

Rivard, Yolande. "Jean Papineau-Couture's Return to Tone Colour."
    The Music Scene, No. 254 (July-August, 1970), p. 4.

PSAUME 150
1954
Jean Papineau-Couture

John Beckwith, in an early 1957 review of Papineau-Couture's **Psaume 150,** said:
". . . undoubtedly one of the finest and most mature works written in Canada in the
past decade (Psalm 150) is gratifying to all who know it. It deserves to become a
classic of our music . . ." And later, in 1969, Andrée Desautels added: "Among the
masterpieces of Couture's first period we would single out the **Concerto Grosso—**
1943; and the **Psaume 150—***1954,* one of his most successful works . . . Occasional
reminders of Stravinsky's **Symphony of Psalms**—harmonic and rhythmic reminiscences—do not detract from Couture's achievement."

As the composer has pointed out, **Psaume 150** is a modern parallel to the Bach
chorale-cantatas where a single chorale is employed in various forms for each of
several movements. In this work, however, the basic tune is an original scalic
motive rather than a hymn melody, or in reality, a tone series. The early-baroque
Venetian school is evident in the scoring of the work, with its antiphonal effects
for concertante winds, brass, organ, and voices. The instrumental and vocal parts
are, as with many of Couture's works, demanding. However, there is an artistry
and a power in the work that gives it a special place in the composer's creative
output.

ANALYSIS:

The work begins with a short organ introduction which is interrupted by a four-measure 'fanfare' of brass. A further seven measures of organ lead into *Alleluia* sung by the four-part choir with orchestral accompaniment. The soprano line (which is the most obvious) is quoted as follows:

Example 1:

At the conclusion of a seven-fold *Alleluia* by the choir, the soprano soloist enters singing the *Alleluia*. At the fourth *Alleluia,* the tenor soloist joins in duet with the soprano — for a seven-fold *Alleluia*. The choir immediately resumes its four-part opening phrases which then lead into a recapitulation of the organ introduction. Next follows a setting of the *Laudate Dominum*. Accompanied by a flute and bassoon, the opening measures are scored for three-part womens' voices; Soprano I, Soprano II, and Alto. In $\frac{5}{4}$ meter, the opening phrases in open score are:

Example 2:

Moving into a *Lento* section, the tenor soloist continues *Laudate eum in virtu-ti-bus ejus* accompanied by brass.

Example 3:

104

Section four commences *Allegro* with a jubilant organ accompaniment built on ascending fourths and descending scale passages — very reminiscent of Buxtehude's style — over a descending scale in the pedal part.

Example 4:

Basses make their entry with a rhythmical motif, followed by the tenors in duet.

Example 5:

A trio of trumpets creates a mood of excitement as the music builds toward a climax. Followed immediately by organ and brass, the tenors and basses again resume their vocal lines — this time in four-part harmony.

Section five is scored entirely for two woodwinds (flute and bassoon) as an accompaniment for the soprano soloist.

Example 6:

105

Moving immediately into the six th and final section marked *Largo,* the choir sings *Laudate eum in cymbalis* in unison, accompanied by the woodwinds and brass.

Example 7:

Expanding into four-part harmonies, each vocal line is treated *divisi,* and alternates between contrapuntal and chordal textures. Joined shortly by the soprano and then the tenor soloist and organ accompaniment, the music again changes tempo to *Andante.* At this point the opening *Alleluias* are repeated as the movement recapitulates the material heard at the commencement of the work. After reaching a *fortissimo* climax, the *Alleluias* subside in intensity — but only momentarily, for the last three statements of the *Alleluia* treated chordally in augmentation peal out once again, bringing the work to a triumphal ending. This is a most satisfying work, and one which deserves greater recognition and familiarity through repeated performance. The study score, published by BMI, is obtainable from Berandol Music.

PIÈCE CONCERTANTE No.3
1959
Jean Papineau-Couture

The **Pièce concertante No. 3,** sub-titled Variations, was written for flute, clarinet, violin, cello, harp, and string orchestra. The work was commissioned by the Montreal Symphony Orchestra. Dedicated to Igor Markevitch, it was premiered on March 24, 1959, with Markevitch conducting the Montreal Symphony. The third work in a series of five **Pièces concertantes** written by the composer to this date, they collectively represent a distinctive contribution to the Canadian repertoire. With each piece scored for a different *solo/tutti* instrumental combination, they form a significant part of the composer's works from 1957 to 1963.

ANALYSIS:

The work consists of a theme, ten variations, and a fugue. As a group, the solo instruments are often in opposition to the string orchestra. At other moments one finds a single instrument highlighted, while the rest of the soloists lend support to the orchestral accompaniment.

Commencing very slowly, the string orchestra announces the main theme in unison. This is a sixteen measure statement which forms a basis for the entire work. In the first example the twelve chromatic tones are clearly stated.

Example 1:

The first variation commences with the theme divided between the flute and clarinet, accompanied by violin, cello, and harp. Played very softly, the first few measures are as follows:

Example 2: *Variation 1*

The second variation commences with the string basses playing a repeated tone (D) below the harp and clarinet parts. Cello, clarinet, and flute share the variation which is played slowly and softly. The harp also may be heard for a few measures.

107

Example 3: *Variation 2*

Variation three commences in the strings. There is a noticeable dynamic *crescendo* before the strings subside, allowing the soloists to complete the variation.

Example 4: *Variation 3*

The harp introduces the fourth variation. At a slightly faster tempo, occasional comments by individual solo instruments complement the variation.

Example 5: *Variation 4*

The harp continues with a chordal accompaniment in the fifth variation. Against an ascending line for cello, the solo flute announces the theme.

Example 6: *Variation 5*

The sixth variation is played by the strings. An interesting feature is the rhythm created by the use of 3+3+2 sixteenth-notes in each measure.

Example 7: *Variation 6*

Both solo violin and cello announce variation seven in octaves, accompanied by the string orchestra. The music is marked *Risoluto*. A short commentary on flute and clarinet also adds to the orchestral colour.

Example 8: *Variation 7*

Variation eight commences in almost a whisper. Marked *Misterioso*, the solo flute introduces the variation, accompanied by repetitive string chords. The middle phrase in the variation is given to the solo clarinet. The harp chording is almost imperceptible as the flute resumes and completes the variation.

Example 9: *Variation 8*

There is a marked contrast in mood in the last two variations. Variation nine is played vigorously by the string orchestra. The CBC recording omits the first section and commences at letter N, page 26 in the score. At this point, the tempo is very fast and, with repetitive figures in the lower strings, the first violins sound to advantage. This is the theme as played by the first violins in the record released by the CBC.

Example 10: *Variation 9*

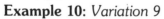

The ninth variation closes with the addition of cello and harp, leading into the final variation. Marked *Largo,* the rhythmic definition is more forceful here than in any previous section. A gradual *crescendo* leads once again to the final measures which subside and conclude quietly.

Example 11: *Variation 10*

At the conclusion of the ten variations, there is a short pause. Immediately the fugue commences with the fugue subject announced on the solo cello. The subject, which consists of all twelve chromatic tones (in the same order as they appeared in the variations), is shown in the following example.

Example 12: *Subject*

The answer follows on the solo clarinet. For students not familiar with fugue form, the answer in the dominant is shown.

Example 13: *Answer*

The third and fourth entries are played by solo violin and flute respectively. Listening carefully to each successive entry in the fugue exposition will reveal not only

110

the melodic and harmonic content but also the individual timbres of woodwind and string instruments.

As the fugue develops, there are several aspects that could assist the listening experience. The distinctive five-note opening of the subject may be heard in the accompanying strings, on harp, and again on various solo instruments.

Papineau-Couture employs the usual fugue devices, which include inversion, augmentation, and diminution, as he gradually builds his orchestral forces into a musical edifice. As each entry reinforces the theme, the music develops its distinctive chromatic quality as it progresses, building the conviction that here is music that epitomizes the originality, sensitivity, artistry, and technique of one of Canada's finest composers.

CONCERTO for PIANO and ORCHESTRA
1965
Jean Papineau-Couture

Papineau-Couture's **Piano Concerto** was commissioned by the Canadian Broadcasting Corporation and first performed on February 6, 1966 in the series "Concerts from Two Worlds." The Toronto Symphony Orchestra was conducted by Alexander Brott and the soloist was Gilles Manny, a young Canadian pianist to whom the work is dedicated. The **Concerto** requires an orchestra of only moderate size. The style is chromatic, not serial. It is not tonal, but also not completely atonal. The work is in one continuous movement with two main motifs, both announced by the piano — the first is at the beginning when the piano plays alone; the second is scherzo-like, about two measures long, repeated often by the piano accompanied by the snare drum.

ANALYSIS:

The opening theme is announced by the piano. It is a seven-measure statement which commences as follows:

Example 1:

Immediately the orchestra is heard in reply — but only for a few measures before the piano resumes its solo passage. Without accompaniment, the piano theme is announced.

Example 2:

This leads immediately into a *Scherzando* motif that has short fragmentary phrases answering in the woodwind and brass.

Example 3:

The two-measure figure will be heard several times as the music returns to the *Scherzando* tempo after excursions into slower and faster tempi. A repetitive figure in the piano propels the music forward, accompanied by short motivic elements in woodwinds, brass, and strings. An example of a brass motif occurs at page 14 in the score.

Example 4:

A *diminuendo* follows with very soft accompanying phrases as the piano dominates the texture. At letter H in the score, there is a short passage for percussion —

woodblocks, cymbals, triangle, and gongs. A noticeable *ritard* leads into a slower section at page 23 in the score. But only momentarily — for the *Scherzando* returns a few measures later. After a significant piano solo which leads toward a climactic point, a trumpet may be heard playing this descending theme in triplets.

Example 5:

This is followed by several quieter phrases with the piano part still dominating the texture in a *quasi-cadenza* styled solo. Repetitions of both melodic and rhythmic elements are noticeable in the solo passage — particularly the *Adagio* theme as illustrated in the second example. Joined a little later by the first violins, the texture continues in three parts with the addition of the violin line. Notice at this point, the three-note descending figure on the piano against the ascending line for first violins.

Example 6:

After several measures of *Adagio,* the *Scherzando* theme (see Example 3) again returns; this time it builds towards a somewhat noisy climax, including in the process an *ostinato* figure on piano. A momentary pause occurs. At this point, bassoon and horns can be heard quietly accompanying the piano. This lyrical figure is then transferred to the strings for a short phrase, leaving the piano solo to dominate. At page 64, a *Meno mosso* played softly changes the mood.

Example 7:

Again the *Scherzando* motif returns. With a gradual thickening of the texture, the music pulsates forward at a head-long pace, finishing abruptly after a very animated and exciting concluding statement by the full orchestra.

ROBERT TURNER

1920

Composer, Professor

Robert Turner belongs to the small company of Canadian composers who were born in Canada, who gained their early musical experience in Canada, and whose musical studies resulted in the conferring of advanced degrees in music by universities in Canada. Apart from short periods of study in England and in the United States, he has spent the greater part of his life working as a teacher, CBC producer, and university professor. At present he is on the Music Faculty of the University of Manitoba, and with his wife Sara and their children, lives in a comfortable home in a suburb of Winnipeg.

Born in Montreal on June 6, 1920, Robert Turner commenced piano lessons at an early age. During his school years, he developed an interest in composition and without any formal instruction began to compose music. More advanced piano studies with Frank Hanson and Walter Hungerford at McGill Conservatory of Music stimulated his interest in composition. While attending high school, he worked with Irvin Cooper of Montreal studying composition and orchestration. Encouraged by Cooper to continue his studies, Turner entered McGill University where he studied composition with Douglas Clarke, and harmony, counterpoint, and composition with Claude Champagne. In 1943 he graduated from McGill with a Bachelor of Music degree. The following two years were spent in service with the RCAF. On his return to civilian life, Turner resumed studies with Douglas Clarke, and in the summer of 1947 he studied composition with Roy Harris at Colorado College. Awarded a scholarship by the Royal College of Music in London, he spent one year (1947-48) studying composition with Herbert Howells and orchestration with Gordon Jacob. Preferring to work with Roy Harris, he moved to Nashville, Tennessee, where he majored in composition at George Peabody College for Teachers under the American composer's guidance. After graduation in 1950 with a Master of Music degree, Turner spent one year teaching in Kentucky (where his wife was timpanist with the Louisville Orchestra), and then returned to Canada to teach music in Kelowna, British Columbia. In 1952, he joined the CBC in Vancouver as music producer. While in Vancouver, he completed the requirements for a Doctorate in Music at McGill University and received this degree in 1953.

Throughout the sixteen years Dr. Turner lived and worked in Vancouver, he composed a significant amount of music. Recognition of his compositional ability led to a number of awards, scholarships, and commissions. In 1960 he received a Canada Council grant resulting in **Symphony for Strings**—*1960;* and **Fantasia**—*1962,* for organ, brass quintet, and timpani. He was awarded a Canada Council Senior Arts Fellowship in 1966-67. During these years, he was in charge of major CBC programs involving 'live' serious music. This included productions by the CBC Vancouver Chamber Orchestra, network recitals of chamber music, and larger productions of opera and oratorio, such as Frank Martin's **Golgotha,** Copland's **Tender Land,** and Barbara Pentland's one-act opera, **The Lake.** In fact classical music, whatever its nature, was Turner's responsibility. In this capacity, he was able to keep in close association with both music and professional performers, and to be involved in decisions affecting the broadcasting of high-quality music.

In the fall of 1968, Dr. Turner moved from Vancouver to a teaching appointment at Acadia University, Nova Scotia. One year later he was appointed to the University of Manitoba, where he now holds the rank of Professor of Theory and Composition. As a member of the Composers' Guild of Great Britain (Western Canada representative), a member of the Canadian League of Composers, and an affiliated member of BMI Canada, he is highly respected. In the December, 1970 issue of *Musicanada,* the Canadian Music Centre chose Robert Turner for their 'Composer's Portrait' which included an up-to-date catalogue of the composer's works. In this list there is an impressive variety of compositions that range from opera to orchestral and chamber works, and to choral, vocal, and keyboard works. Turner's compositions have been written largely as a result of commissions. More than forty works have been composed during the last twenty-five years, and although this output could not be considered prolific, there is a remarkable consistency in the quality of his music — always in good taste, whatever the musical medium may happen to be.

Among his more important works are the following:

1. **String Quartet No. 1**—*1949,* the earliest work in Turner's catalogue. It was first performed at the Berkshire Festival, Tanglewood, under the aegis of Aaron Copland.

2. **Sonatina for Oboe and Piano**—*1951.*

3. **String Quartet No. 2**—*1954,* was composed for the 50th anniversary of the McGill Conservatory of Music.

4. **Opening Night**—*1955,* a theatre overture. This work was published by BMI Canada, premiered by the Vancouver Symphony under Irwin Hoffman in 1955, and recorded by CBC in 1960 and again in 1971.

5. **A Children's Overture**—*1958,* recorded by CBC, released by London Records.

6. **Six Voluntaries for Organ**—*1959.*

7. **Variations and Toccata**—*1959.*

8. **Symphony for Strings**—*1960,* recorded by the CBC, and released jointly by the CBC and RCA Victor under the label Music and Musicians of Canada.

9. **The Phoenix and the Turtle**—*1964,* for voice and eight instruments, commissioned by the CBC for the Shakespeare Quadricentenary.

10. **Diversities**—*1967,* for violin, bassoon, and piano, commissioned by the Cassenti players on a grant from the Centennial commission, and premiered at the Vancouver Festival and at Expo '67, in Montreal.

11. **The Brideship**—*1967,* a lyric drama of three scenes in one act, especially commissioned by the CBC for the Centennial year.

12. **Trio for Violin, Cello, and Piano**—*1969.*

Has the change in role from CBC producer to university professor affected in any noticeable way the style or content of Turner's music? Perhaps it is a little early to fully assess and accurately answer this question. One could describe such early works as **Symphony for Strings** and **Six Voluntaries for Organ** as conservative in style, when compared to the currently fashionable sounds that emanate from some of our more avant-garde composers. As yet the listener must wait for either the CBC or commercial recording companies to record and release newer compositions such as **Nostalgia** for soprano saxophone and piano—*1972;* or the recent **Chamber Concerto for Bassoon and 17 Instruments**—*1973,* commissioned by George Zukerman. The most recent recordings of Turner's music include the CBC Radio Canada releases of the **Serenade for Woodwind Quintet**—*1960;* **Fantasy and Festivity for Harp**—*1970,* a work commissioned by the CBC, composed for and dedicated to the harpist Judy Loman; and **Eidolons**—*1972*, a work described as 'Twelve Images for Chamber Orchestra', commissioned by the CBC for the CBC Vancouver Chamber Orchestra. Certainly in these works, one hears many exciting colouristic effects and a careful juxtaposition of traditional and contemporary styles.

Another recent composition which may be destined to be one of the composer's most important works to date is the **Concerto for Two Pianos and Orchestra**—*1971*. Commissioned by the duo pianists Garth Beckett and Boyd McDonald, it was first performed on January 22nd, 1972, at the Manitoba Centennial Hall, Winnipeg, with the Winnipeg Symphony Orchestra under Piero Gamba. Discussing the performance, Madeleine Bernier wrote in the *Winnipeg Tribune:* "The **Concerto,** strictly in the contemporary idiom, is undergirded by modes prevalent in the Middle Ages. It utilizes several folk tunes and melodies. Most of these are disguised through alterations made on the original rhythms, by transposition into a different mode, or by altering the note combinations of a given melody. It took extremely proficient artists to brilliantly combine all these elements." Ronald Gibson reported in the *Winnipeg Free Press:* "Dr. Turner's music turned out to be quite capable of comprehension. It has charm, and its orchestration was at times captivating."

A fascinating work which departs somewhat from Turner's usual style is his Christmas music, **Johann's Gift to Christmas**—*1972*. Requiring a narrator and orchestra, the libretto was written by Jack Richards of the *Vancouver Sun*. Discussing the first performance by the Vancouver Symphony Orchestra at the Vancouver Queen Elizabeth Theatre, Max Wyman of the *Vancouver Sun* commented: "A memorable and atmospheric experience . . . 'Johann's Gift to Christmas' is more mood than action, and told in a lovely tender way that has been marvellously matched by Turner. He draws us a sound picture of the Austria of 150 years ago that parallels and enhances the word picture that Richards has drawn. Everything that Turner does neatly epitomizes the feel of the tale in the same gentle way that the words do."

Robert Turner has been described as a rather shy, slow-spoken man, and not one you would think likely to influence a large public. This may be one's first impression of him, but his close associates know him to be a man with a strong sense of purpose — a man who composes music of integrity and craftsmanship. Professor Peter Garvie in a short summary of Turner's music made the following pertinent comments: "Robert Turner's output is thoughtful and distinguished. His music has no dogmatic allegiance (he uses serial techniques freely when it suits him), but nourishes its roots in human experience and its power to communicate directly. It can be gay without being slick, and deeply felt without losing balance and clarity. These are considerable gifts . . ."

A variety of musical forms and styles are included in Turner's works. He has successfully composed attractive and popular pieces such as the **Opening Night** overture, and **Robbins Round** (a third-stream work in the form of a concertino for jazz band), as naturally as he has created his mature orchestral and chamber works. His personal preference is to write works in free forms such as those found in the fantasia. Although he has composed in the traditional sonata form, very few of his works are similar in design. Apart from the two string quartets, all the remaining compositions are cast in different forms and require differing combinations of instruments resulting in timbres and textures which are excitingly unique. Although a rather strict adherent to the twelve-tone method during the ten year period 1959-69, he has now noticeably departed from this method in his latest works. His **Trio for Violin, Cello, and Piano**—*1969,* composed for the Trio Victoria, could be considered a transitional work in this regard. The first movement, written in strict serial style, is followed by a passacaglia in the second movement; however, the third movement (a recapitulation of material used earlier) is treated more freely, resulting at times in a tonal treatment of the row. Since this work, the composer has become more eclectic in his approach. Serialism has not been abandoned, but the freedom to use whatever resources are needed is probably an indication of the composer's growing maturity.

When questioned about future hopes and aspirations, Dr. Turner reemphasized his interest in literature and drama. He enjoyed writing **The Brideship,** a lyric drama, and commenced work on a full-length opera during his sabbatical year 1975-76. In collaboration with Norman Newton, a CBC producer who wrote the libretto, the story is a modern version of the Hippolytus legend set on Vancouver Island during the nineteen-twenties and should provide a fascinating challenge. In a discussion of the proposed work, the composer indicated that he would utilize a more eclectic approach without any fixed adherence to one method of writing. He will make use of whatever means he thinks would be effective. Obviously, a work of this magnitude will take a year or two to complete. He is currently writing a work to be performed by the Vancouver Symphony. Commissioned especially by the CBC, the work will feature cellist Zara Nelsova and pianist Grant Johannesen.

Most of Robert Turner's music has been composed as a result of commissions. He does not write a work and then look for a publisher or performer. The specific requirements of a Canada Council or CBC commission are sufficient to inspire. If a work is published or recorded, it is because it is recognized for its quality and its ability to sustain interest in performer and listener alike. The variety of his music and the favourable reception new works receive from the musical public indicate a promising future for a composer of sincerity and integrity, one who has made a lasting contribution to the music of this century.

REFERENCES

Garvie, Peter. "Robert Turner." *The Music Scene,* No. 245
(January-February, 1969), p. 9.

"Robert Turner." *Compositores de América/Composers of the Americas,*
Vol. 5 (1959), pp. 98-102.

"Robert Turner — A Portrait." *Musicanada,* No. 29 (1970), pp. 10-11.

"Robert Turner." *Biographies of Canadian Composers,*
CBC International Service (1964), pp. 98-100.

"Robert Turner." *Baker's Biographical Dictionary of Musicians*
(1971), p. 1670, (Supplement, p. 243).

OPENING NIGHT
A Theatre Overture
1955
Robert Turner

Opening Night was commissioned by the Vancouver Symphony Society in 1955 and given its first performance that year by the Vancouver Symphony Orchestra conducted by Irwin Hoffman. The work is scored for full orchestra and its overall form is basically three part (ABA). Generally, the music is festive and rhythmic and meant to convey the mood of excitement, anticipation, and glamour that surrounds an opening night in the theatre. There is much use of syncopation and the piece evolves practically its entire thematic material from the germinal motif contained in its first two measures. In the third section (recapitulation), the initial notes of "From Leicester Square to Old Broadway" (theme song of a popular Vancouver radio series) are heard played by the piccolo and later by the trombones.

ANALYSIS:

The movement begins with a syncopated fanfare in quadruple time played *Allegro e ritmico*. The first two measures, containing the germinal ideas for the entire overture, are quoted for our consideration.

Example 1:

It will be noticed that the opening measure is played by the brass and answered immediately by the timpani. Notice the contemporary harmony produced by superimposing the D major chord over the chord of E-flat major. The entire introductory statement of 36 measures continues with the strongly-syncopated style indicated in the opening measures. At the twelfth measure, the woodwinds announce a theme that becomes important in later development.

Example 2:

After a slight ritard the strings announce a new theme. This thematic material, of utmost importance to the movement, will be heard in a variety of presentations.

Example 3:

This initial statement is again heard (six measures later) played by the full orchestra in transposed positions.

Example 4:

With several repetitions of the theme by group and individual instruments, Example 4 reappears in the strings. Notice the rearrangement of motifs from their original presentation as shown in Example 3.

Example 5:

As the music continues, theme two reappears played by the full orchestra against syncopated rhythms. Without any break in the music, Section B commences. Here the tempo directions are *ma molto leggiero*. The oboe announces a quiet theme against a *pizzicato* string accompaniment.

Example 6:

This theme is continued by the flute and later by the clarinet and bassoon above sixteenth-note figurations in the strings. As the theme develops, the brass may be heard against a sustained lyrical accompaniment. As the music moves into a *molto tranquillo* section, tubular bells are heard accompanying sustained woodwinds and *pizzicato* strings. Here the violas have the theme transposed to another pitch.

Example 7:

Vla.

A slight pause precedes the reappearance of the thematic material referred to in Example 6. This time, however, the theme is played by the clarinet rather than the oboe and is heard one semi-tone higher.

Example 8:

Clarinet
in C

Against strongly-syncopated rhythms, the brass predominate as the middle section approaches the recapitulation. A few measures of soft woodwinds follow, leading quite naturally into the recapitulation.

At this point, Section A is repeated, beginning with theme three (excluding the introductory statements referred to in Examples 1 and 2). With effective use of the percussion section, the recapitulation continues in a vigorous and deliberate mood. Emphatic statements in the brass add brilliance and excitement as the festive mood builds towards a climax. Quite suddenly a lively piccolo solo is heard reminiscing on the popular tune 'From Leicester Square to Old Broadway.'

Example 9:

Piccolo

A few measures later, the trombones also "sing" the melody. With the strings playing sixteenth-note figures against the bold brass, the music is propelled vigorously towards the concluding measures. Several sharp percussive chords climax the work, bringing to conclusion a concert overture that deserves frequent hearing.

125

VARIATIONS and TOCCATA
1959
Robert Turner

This work was commissioned by the University of Saskatchewan for its Golden Jubilee Music Festival. It was first performed by the Festival Chamber Group, under Murray Adaskin, in July, 1959. The scoring is for ten instruments: flute, oboe, clarinet, bassoon, horn, two violins, viola, cello, and double-bass.

The two movements are played without a break. The *Variations* are built on two twelve-tone rows — the first constructed of four three-note segments (original, inversion, retrograde, retrograde inversion), and the second derived from the first by taking every second note. This basic material is treated in a free manner and within a tonal framework. The tonal centre of the work is A and the twelve variations follow closely, as in a chaconne, each in a tonality a semi-tone lower (A, Ab, G, Gb, etc.) leading directly into the *Toccata* with the return of A. Fast and rhythmic, the *Toccata* winds up the work in a lighter mood, in contrast to the *Variations* which are rather intense and dramatic.

ANALYSIS:
The tone-row on which the work is based is presented as follows:

Example 1:

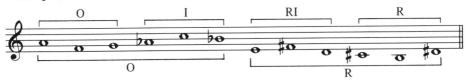

Cleverly constructed, the second part of the row is the retrograde of the original. The second tone-row utilized by the composer is derived from the original by selecting every alternate note, thus producing a new series.

Example 2:

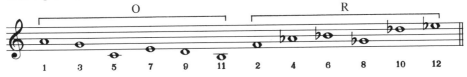

Using both rows, the composer constructs the set of variations, beginning with an introductory statement which is presented as follows.

Example 3:

It will be noticed that the opening section states the original row, splitting it between the individual strings. Using the inversion of the first three-note cell, the woodwinds make their appearance. Each woodwind entry is derived from the row by using one of the possible transformations of the row.

Example 4:

The first variation centres on A and commences in the clarinet with a *pizzicato* accompaniment in the strings.

127

Example 5: *Variation 1*

The second variation, *Più agitato,* consists of another eight measures strongly syncopated in nature. This leads into the third variation, *Risoluto,* (again a semitone lower) also strongly syncopated and with considerable movement in the lower parts. The fourth variation consists of very soft strings accompanying oboe, bassoon, clarinet, and horn episodes.

Example 6: *Variation 4*

Variation 5, *Piangendo,* is also a quietly-moving miniature that features the woodwinds over a sustained pedal tone on E. A short but powerful *cadenza* (still over the E pedal tone) immediately follows, and leads directly into Variation 6, entitled *Feroce.* Here the solo violin continues its thirty-second-note patterns against strongly punctuated chords.

Esaltato is the indication given to the seventh variation. Clarinet, oboe, bassoon, and horn present a chordal progression accompanied by a quickly moving flute *obbligato.* Strings also remain in the background. The eighth variation, *Molto sostenuto,* presents a fuller orchestral tone with all ten instruments playing together. In Variation 9, the oboe is heard above the remaining orchestration.

Example 7: *Variation 9*

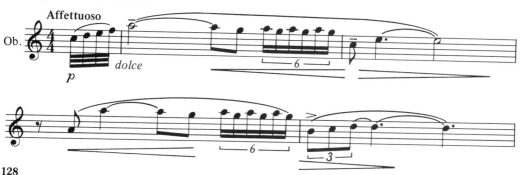

Variation 10, *Soave,* is a little slower in tempo and continues much as before with the accent on the woodwinds. A change in style and mood accompanies Variation 11, *Precipitando.* The eight measures consist entirely of a fast-moving string passage which leads immediately into the last variation, *Allegro vigoroso.* With a change to compound duple meter, the variation maintains the same vigorous string tone, accompanied by short woodwind interjections. Without a score, one would be uncertain of the exact commencement of the *Toccata,* as the last variation leads directly into the second movement without a break. The strings, however, play the opening statement and, four measures later, the horn may be heard assisting.

Example 8:

The spirited mood is continued at a fast and rhythmical tempo in duple meter. At letter B, as shown in Example 9, a slight tempo change is noticeable as the flute and clarinet play a short duet above the five-note rhythmical violin figure.

Example 9:

The lighter mood of the *Toccata* persists, in contrast to the earlier *Variations.* This is particularly evident with the several brief appearances of individual instruments, as each gaily adds its own contribution. A brief appearance of the strings alone occurs at page 49 in the score. Here the viola and second violin play a short phrase together. The viola leads with six measures before the entry of the violin.

Example 10:

Notice the ascending and descending string lines. Augmented by the remaining instrumental ensemble, the music moves ahead full of vitality and vigour. Finally there is a noticeable *rallentando* — complete with pause — and then one short burst of life brings the work to a very satisfying conclusion. Completed on May 24, 1959, in Vancouver, B.C., the **Variations and Toccata** adds immeasurably to the growing list of significant Canadian compositions.

SERENADE for WOODWIND QUINTET
1960
Robert Turner

The **Serenade for Woodwind Quintet** was written by Turner as a result of a CBC commission in 1960. It is a one-movement work consisting of five sections: *Scherzando, March, Adagio, Waltz,* and *Scherzando.* Composed in a strictly twelve-tone idiom, the *Serenade* is a welcome addition to the available literature for woodwind quintet. The CBC recording of the Vancouver Woodwind Quintet's performance in the Recital Hall at the University of British Columbia is a good one, and faithfully reproduces the composer's intentions.

ANALYSIS:

The work is scored for the usual quintet — flute, oboe, clarinet, horn, and bassoon. The *Scherzando* presents opportunities for each instrument to be heard in both solo and accompanying roles. The opening statement consists of a short dialogue between the oboe and *staccato* accompanying instruments. Here is the oboe line.

Example 1:

Short melodic phrases strongly syncopated in nature follow — first on the oboe, then flute, bassoon, horn, and clarinet. A triplet figure is introduced on the bassoon and then tossed to the horn.

Example 2:

With an alternation of homophonic and polyphonic textures, the introductory section is propelled forward through a series of phrases — repetitious in nature, but differing in instrumental timbres. Against a chordal progression, the bassoon plays a melody derived from the opening example.

131

Example 3:

Imitative phrases follow, and a return to the sharp *staccato* accompaniment brings the *Scherzando* to its conclusion.

The *March* begins after a slight pause. Distinctive characteristics include a faster tempo in duple meter, and a rhythmic pulsation provided by the bassoon. A five-note rhythmic pattern helps to maintain the same percussive *staccato* quality. Four sharp *staccato* chords precede the oboe solo shown in Example 4.

Example 4:

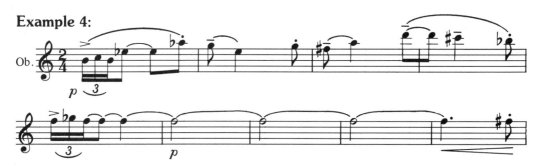

Imitated immediately by the bassoon, the short section rapidly builds toward a climax. At this point the *Adagio* begins. The flute leads, with the oboe following in canon one measure later.

Example 5:

Imitative phrases follow on all instruments, creating opportunities for the listener to detect the characteristic timbres and the polyphonic textures of this middle section. The lyrical nature of the *Adagio* is also in marked contrast to the sections which precede and follow.

Moving immediately into the *Waltz* section, a flute solo consisting of a repetitive two-measure figure is accompanied by the remaining quartet.

Example 6:

Variants on this theme are then tossed to each of the other members of the quintet. With a strong triple rhythm, the music develops to a *crescendo* and stops abruptly. At this point the last 24 measures of the *Scherzando* reappear in the form of a recapitulation. With clearly articulated rhythms, the music builds toward a dynamic climax and then quietly subsides, concluding on one soft *staccato* chord.

Music of this nature offers exceptional opportunities to develop discrimination in each of the five basic elements of music — rhythm, melody, harmony, tone colour, and form. The transparent lines create textures and timbres which are easily definable as are the rhythmic and melodic elements. Familiarity with the music through several repetitions should aid the listener in gaining a better understanding, and a greater appreciation of the musical content.

THE CARRION CROW
1973
Robert Turner

This song is the third in a group of five Canadian folksongs (from the Maritimes and Newfoundland) especially arranged for unaccompanied mixed chorus by Robert Turner, as a result of a commission by the Canadian Broadcasting Corporation in 1973. **The Carrion Crow** was obtained originally from *Maritime Folksongs* collected by Helen Creighton and published by McGraw-Hill Ryerson Limited.

At the present time, the collection of *5 Canadian Folksongs* remains unpublished. However, a copy of the completed score is located at the Canadian Music Centre, Toronto. The experience of rehearsing **Carrion Crow** in a high school music class may effectively demonstrate the composer's treatment of the original folk-tune in a four-part setting for mixed chorus.

The Carrion Crow

135

HARRY FREEDMAN
1922
Composer

Most composers find it necessary to spend a large proportion of their time teaching or performing music. This division of their energy may seriously affect the quality and quantity of their creative output. In this respect, Harry Freedman is very unusual, for, since his retirement as an instrumentalist with the Toronto Symphony Orchestra in 1970, he has devoted all his time and skill to musical composition. Supported by commissions, he has firmly established an enviable reputation as a fine craftsman — a composer who is recognized as one of Canada's most musically articulate.

Harry Freedman was born in Lodz, Poland, on April 5th, 1922. When he was three, his parents immigrated to Canada, settling at first in Medicine Hat, Alberta, and later in Winnipeg, Manitoba. During his school years he did not receive music lessons; however, he did develop a strong interest in both art and music — particularly jazz music. In fact, his love for jazz eventually prompted him at eighteen years of age to purchase a clarinet and commence lessons with Arthur Hart of Winnipeg.

Freedman's musical career was prefaced by service with the RCAF during World War II. Throughout the major part of this period he played in Canadian Air Force bands, gaining experience as a performer — at first on clarinet and later on oboe. On his return to civilian life, he settled in Toronto with the express purpose of studying music at the Toronto (now Royal) Conservatory of Music. During this five year period, he studied oboe with Perry Bauman and twelve-tone composition with John Weinzweig. In 1946, he joined the Toronto Symphony Orchestra as English horn soloist. Throughout his long association with the Toronto Symphony and the Canadian Broadcasting Corporation's Symphony Orchestra, he expanded his musical horizons by studying composition with three world-renowned composers, Ernest Krenek, Olivier Messiaen, and Aaron Copland.

For a composer who has spent a large proportion of his life as a professional performer, Harry Freedman's catalogue of compositions is impressive, spanning a period of almost thirty years. In addition to his performing and composing, he has supported the Toronto Musicians Association, is a member of CAPAC and an active member of the Canadian League of Composers, and is at present on the Board of Directors of the Canadian Music Centre. Recognition of his musical ability is also evident in the form of scholarships and Canada Council grants.

Freedman's creative ability has also been directed in more recent years to works suitable for educational purposes. His association with North York and the Scarborough Boards of Education, as a composer in the classroom, has resulted in numerous works specifically written for high school bands and orchestras. These works, along with his many radio, television, and motion picture scores, reveal a composer of imagination and vitality who is particularly gifted and able to communicate with young audiences of today. Discussing his involvement with school music, the composer is quoted in *The Canadian Composer* (December, 1974) as saying: "For several years I've been working on a project; it's like a **Mikrokosmos** for school band that eventually will be about 200 pieces, starting from the very first lesson where every instrument is playing one note. Instead of the usual band method, where everybody starts on the same note, say Eb, my idea is that every instrument starts on its easiest note, so immediately you have texture instead of unison. In one of the pieces, I've written a section where a little element of chance creeps in and the kids loved it. That's been the one they've wanted to do most." This aspect of the composer's educational interest is further expanded in an article entitled "Freedman in the Classroom," published in the September, 1974 issue of *The Recorder,* the Ontario Music Educators' Association journal.

Freedman's ability to communicate is due in part to his own awareness of the changing society in which we live. Discussing this particular Freedman characteristic in the April,1967 edition of *The Canadian Composer,* Bryan Wilkinson states: "He still retains a characteristic receptivity to change and the new versatility he now exercises within the scope of his musical activity may well be one of the factors that put him among Canada's most exciting composers." Freedman's versatility has been quite pronounced in his own personal and musical life. While making preparations for a career in art, he switched at the age of eighteen years to music; beginning a study of the clarinet, he later changed to oboe and again to the English horn. An established solo performer in Toronto, he relinquished his position as a full-time performer and is now fully occupied in musical composition. Among his many interests in composition is his 1970 appointment as Composer-in-Residence to the Toronto Symphony Orchestra — an appointment believed to be the first of its kind to be made by a Canadian symphony orchestra. For him, the future is not a previously-mapped-out road that remains to be travelled. "I'll be looking forward to doing more commissioned works in the future, of course, but apart from that I can't say which way my work will go, except that I'll do what appeals to me at the time."

In a more recent interview with the composer (quoted in *The Canadian Composer,* December, 1974), Michael Schulman reveals some of the influences that have shaped Harry Freedman's musical outlook and direction. "My interest in composing came from jazz, long before I joined the Toronto Symphony, because in jazz, the performer is the creator. Everything I have been as a composer has come from jazz. Duke Ellington is still the most meaningful influence of all." Another major factor in Freedman's musical experience has been the impact of art on his music. He explains it this way: "I see music — colour, shapes. It's a strange thing and I don't know how it happens, but if I look at a painting, I can hear music, and vice versa, musical sounds suggest lines and shapes. It goes way back to my adolescence when I was studying at the Winnipeg School of Art and I was first becoming interested in jazz. I remember thinking, wouldn't it be terrific to paint sort of abstract things in the styles of all these jazz musicians." ". . . when my interest in jazz and music became so intense, I turned around and thought, gee, wouldn't it be great to compose a piece that interpreted different paintings?" As we will discover later, this interest in art resulted in the creation of **Images**—*1957-58,* a most popular and often-performed composition.

Freedman has composed successfully in all genres except opera. Probably he is best known for his orchestral music, which includes five ballets choreographed by Brian MacDonald. He has also written scores for Stratford Festival Shakespearian productions, radio and television shows, and the films *Act of the Heart* (for which he won the Etrog Canadian film award) and *The Pyx.* His full-length ballet *Rose Latulippe,* composed on a centennial commission for the Royal Winnipeg Ballet, was premiered at Stratford in August 1966. Later, in 1967, it won wide acclaim when televised over the CBC network by the Ballet company. The composer has also written background music for many CBC films and documentaries, among them *Pale Horse, Pale Rider; 700 Million; Romeo and Jeannette;* and *The Dark Will Not Conquer.* Another most successful work is the composer's *Tangents* (symphonic variations) commissioned by the National Youth Orchestra Association and played to young audiences across Canada. Performed several times by the Toronto Symphony Orchestra under Seiji Ozawa, it has also received performances in the U.S.A.; at the Festival Hall, London; at Lyons City Theatre, France; and at Expo '67 in Montreal.

Of particular interest to audiences are a number of specific compositions selected from his catalogue for their appeal. **Nocturne**—*1949* for orchestra, was first performed in 1952 in Toronto at the Canadian League of Composers concert and later recorded by the CBC with the Toronto Orchestra under Geoffrey Waddington. **Tableau**—*1952* for string orchestra, commissioned by Forest Hill Community Centre and published by G. Ricordi, was also performed in 1952 in Toronto by the Canadian Chamber Players under Victor Feldbrill and recorded in 1956 by CBC Strings under Thomas Mayer. **Tableau** was an important milestone in Freedman's development, for it is a work in which he really felt his student days were in the past. Commenting on the music, Freedman said: "When I finished **Tableau,** I knew I was a composer . . . I really knew then that I was no longer a student. I knew that I had created something that although strongly influenced by Bartok (which is very apparent), it is not Bartok — it is all twelve-tone music, and it did what I set out to do with it." In 1953-54 the **Two Vocalises** for soprano, clarinet, and piano were written. Performed many times by his wife Mary Morrison (one of Canada's leading professional soprano soloists), they have become well-known and useful additions to the contemporary literature for soprano voice, clarinet, and piano. Certainly more copies are sold of this work than of any other composed by Freedman. During the 1950's, the composer moved away from twelve-tone composition. **Images**—*1958* was not twelve-tone and appears in retrospect to be a culmination of a period where serialism was temporarily put aside. In the 1960's, however, there is a noticeable return to twelve-tone technique. His 1965 composition, the **Variations** for flute, oboe, and harpsichord; and **Tangents** — symphonic variations—*1967,* were both serially constructed.

Discussing his use of the twelve-tone technique, Harry Freedman commented: "I was never really taken with the idea of a total serial composition in which everything — every single element is accounted for by the row. **Tangents** is really typical of everything I write, in that there are variations not only of the theme, but they follow the general principle that I follow in all my music; I try for the perfect balance between unity and variety . . . unity and variety as applied to the four basic elements of music — pitch, timbre, amplitude, and duration. These are the four things that are always paramount in my mind. And there is texture which is tremendously important; much more important than where the note is."

Other significant music composed over the last decade would include **Tokaido**—*1964* for choir and woodwind quintet, commissioned and performed by the Festival Singers of Canada; **Klee Wyck**—*1970* for full orchestra, commissioned and first performed by the Victoria Symphony Orchestra under Laszlo Gati in British

Columbia's Centennial year 1971; **Graphic I** *(Out of Silence)—1971* for full orchestra and electronic tape, commissioned and performed by the Toronto Symphony Orchestra in 1971 under the baton of Karel Ancerl. According to the composer, ". . . the idea was to write a work that was quiet — to see how much variety could be achieved within the parameters of very soft dynamics." A work written for alto saxophone, electric bass guitar, and orchestra in 1970 was **Scenario.** Performed in Toronto under Meredith Davies for a CBC Festival, it is described by Freedman as 'pure jazz'. Writing in this idiom is not difficult, for the composer has spent many of his earlier years playing in a number of popular jazz groups. In many respects he parallels Copland in this ability.

Two other pieces written in 1971 were **Keewaydin** and **Tikki Tikki Tembo. Keewaydin** is for SSA and has an optional prepared electronic tape. This work, written for the girls choir of Bishop Strachan School, Toronto, and published by G. V. Thompson, may be heard on a CAPAC (Polydor) record, sung by the Festival Singers. Performed now by many groups across the country, it is 'the closest thing to the hit parade' that Freedman has ever written. **Tikki Tikki Tembo** was written for the Toronto Symphony Orchestra's season of children's concerts. For narrator and woodwind quintet, it is especially suitable for young children. A CBC International Service record has recently been made and most likely will be obtainable shortly through the Canadian Collection. More recent works include **Graphic II— 1972** for string quartet, commissioned by the Purcell String Quartet in Vancouver; and **Quartet—1973** for trombones, and bassoons or cellos. Another very successful work is **Tapestry,** commissioned by the National Arts Centre Orchestra in 1973. This work was composed entirely on material taken from the music of J. S. Bach.

At present, Harry Freedman is working on a setting for soprano with wind quintet, and baritone with brass quartet. These two pieces may be played separately, but they may also be performed together. A recently completed work is entitled **Nocturne II,** an atonal (not twelve-tone) composition commissioned by the Calgary Symphony Orchestra. Discussing this new music, Harry Freedman observed: "Although there are twelve-tone elements in the work, more and more, whenever I use the row I use it as a source for material rather than as a unifying element." In this respect it is possible to distinguish a completely different approach to serialism from that employed by his one-time teacher, John Weinzweig.

Future plans for Harry Freedman will depend on the diverse nature and requirements of commission assignments. He does hope one day to write a large work in the form of a concerto — perhaps a jazz work for someone like Gerry Mulligan. If indeed he undertakes such a commission, there is little doubt that he is able and well-equipped to compose such a work. Freedman would also like to do some settings of Dennis Lee's poems, and he would like very much to reach a point in his career where he could be more selective in his assignments, choosing works where he does not always have such a rush to meet deadlines. Whether the music be written for voice, piano, band, orchestra, or any other medium the composer chooses, Freedman's works are heard more frequently than ever before. His continuing list of commissioned works is certainly indicative of the musical stature which he has achieved in the eyes of the musical public. As he is a relatively young composer, the future holds many opportunities for this truly Canadian artist to continue writing music that speaks not only to Canadians but to a worldwide public.

REFERENCES

"Harry Freedman." *Compositores de América/Composers of the Americas,*
     Vol. 8 (1962), pp. 71-74.

"Harry Freedman — A Portrait." *Musicanada,* No. 8
     (January-February, 1968), pp. 8-9.

Schulman, Michael. "Harry Freedman." *The Canadian Composer/
     Le Compositeur Canadien,* No. 96 (December, 1974), pp. 4-10.

Wilkinson, Bryan. "Harry Freedman: An Exciting Composer."
     The Canadian Composer/Le Compositeur Canadien,
     No. 17 (April, 1967), pp. 4, 36, 46.

IMAGES
1958
Harry Freedman

Written in 1957-58 for the McGill Chamber Ensemble on a commission from the Lapitsky Foundation, **Images,** says the composer, "are musical impressions of three Canadian paintings. But they are not so much concerned with the subject-matter of the paintings as with the line, colour, form, and mood of each; they are, in short, an attempt at translating into musical terms the style of each of the three artists."

Harry Freedman's **Images** is a musical description of paintings by Lawren Harris, Kazuo Nakamura, and Jean-Paul Riopelle. Writing about the music in the *London Sunday Times,* music critic Felix Aprahamian said: "A score one would gladly hear again. The three panels form striking contrasts revealing considerable mastery of orchestral colour and a true feeling for texture. The shapely thematic material is convincingly treated, and the dissonances and wide dynamic contrasts of the finale are as purposeful as the more ingratiating sounds of the two earlier sections."

Freedman's choice of subject for **Images** reflects the composer's early ambition to become a painter himself. It was when studying at the Winnipeg School of Art that the similarity between music and painting first occurred to him. "I remember," quoting directly from *The Canadian Composer,* "being obsessed with the idea of a series of paintings presenting my visual impressions of the styles of several composers and jazz musicians. This changed to another idea, that of composing music based on the styles of famous painters or paintings. I still recognize these early interests as the predominant influences in my attitude to music."

Possessing both visual and aural sensitivity, it is understandable that Harry Freedman is able to draw inspiration from paintings. The first, *Blue Mountain* (Lake and Mountain, 1927) suggests that the composer became a landscape painter in sound; the contours of the mountain are alluded to, with angular melodic lines scored for English horn, bass clarinet, bassoons, French horn, trombone, and low strings — all evoking the sombre lines of the picture. The second painting, Nakamura's *Structure at Dusk,* is quite different from the preceding one. With fragmented lines moving over a background of trills and quietly murmuring strings, the music reflects the lightness and transparency that one associates with oriental art. The third painting, *Landscape,* is an abstract work by Riopelle. This work suggests to the composer the bold and aggressive lines which depict the artist's brush strokes. Fierce passages of wide dynamic contrasts complete the picture in sound, producing a triptych of musical subtlety and power. Freedman's style — frugal and forthright — and his well-trained ear and cultured taste for orchestration enable him to successfully capture in sound that elusive quality that identifies this work as distinctly Canadian. Discussing this view-point as early as 1961 in *The Canadian Music Journal,* Udo Kasemets said of Freedman: ". . . he has all the makings of becoming a prominent figure on the Canadian scene, especially since he has captured in his music much of the spiritual atmosphere of this country."

ANALYSIS:

Movement I—*Blue Mountain* (Lawren Harris)
The opening measures of this movement are very impressive. Commencing very softly on a sustained chord in the low woodwinds, the texture is gradually thickened until at measure seven a two-note rhythm figure is loudly proclaimed (four times), and then allowed to subside.

Example 1:

A melody for the first violins emerges from this introduction. The second violins join in after four measures and they weave a two-strand melody in a high register.

Example 2:

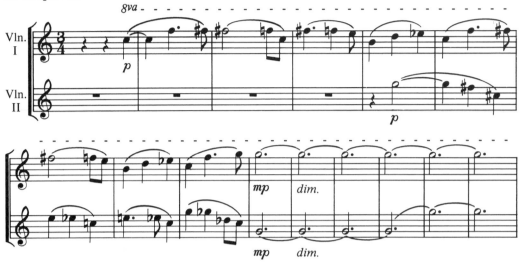

Against sustained high notes in the strings, the English horn may be heard, accompanied by a repeated chord on the vibraphone.

Example 3:

With successive entries in the brass, woodwinds, and strings, the music again builds toward a climax whereupon the original two-note figure is repeated — first by the full orchestra, then by the brass, the strings, and the woodwinds.

Example 4:

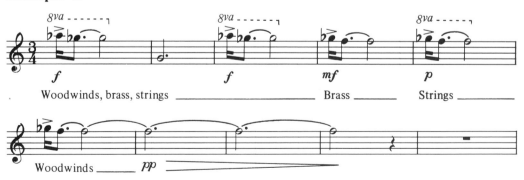

146

An imitative melodic figure commences in the strings at this point (score, page 9).

Example 5:

Again the music develops in intensity as it moves towards a third repetition of the original two-note figure. This time, however, the strings continue with their own independent motif, adding dramatically to the power of the music. With descending melodic contours in the strings becoming slower and softer, the last few measures of the movement gradually fade, but not before the woodwinds and solo strings make their brief appearance.

Movement II—*Structure at Dusk* (Kazuo Nakamura)
This movement is an exquisite example of transparent lines moving over a background of softly murmuring strings. With fragmented lines almost continually in flight, the woodwinds announce their presence, accompanied by the muted trilling of double-stopped strings. The opening measures present the string accompaniment.

Example 6:

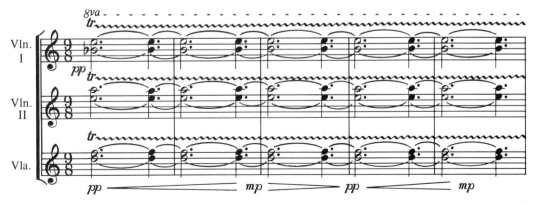

Example 7 presents woodwind motifs — flutes, oboes, and clarinets in succession.

Example 7:

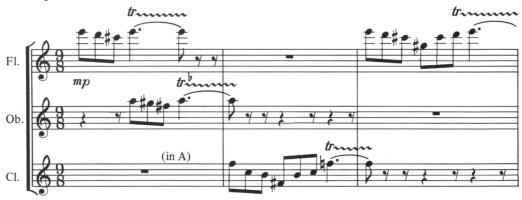

Moving swiftly, the woodwinds present thematic material, while the strings continue their shimmering accompaniment in the background. A short four-measure figure played *pizzicato* on cellos and basses prefaces a return of the trilling strings.

Example 8:

Passing through a wide dynamic range, the wind instruments alternate the trilling figures with the strings as an accompaniment to the thematic development. Approximately halfway through the movement (score, page 26) there is a repetition of Example 8, accompanied by shimmering woodwinds. A short development of this triplet pattern continues exclusively in the strings.

Example 9:

With additional brief commentaries in both woodwind and brass, the music is propelled forward through a series of duple and triple (compound) figurations, both repetitive and scale-like, leading to the conclusion of the delicate movement.

148

Movement III—*Landscape* (Riopelle)

The opening statement consists of a sustained chord cluster from which emerges an ascending figuration.

Example 10:

The initial cluster of notes is in effect, F—G-flat—G-natural.

Example 11:

The movement, written in quadruple meter, is scored alternatively for loud and soft passages. At measure eleven, a repetition of the opening statement occurs with the chord cluster built on D, a minor third lower.

Example 12:

A noticeable feature of each phrase is the immediate dynamic 'build-up' followed by a sudden return to *pianissimo,* to commence the next phrase. The bass clarinet and contra-bassoon commence a two-strand melody at page 47 in the score.

Example 13:

Again this leads into an immediate *crescendo* built on a chord cluster of minor seconds. A soft string passage emerges from this phrase (score, page 49), complemented by short utterances from the bass woodwinds.

Example 14:

After a further characteristic *crescendo,* in which the somewhat dissonant chord cluster is repeated six times, a passage for strings emerges with the second violins commencing the phrase.

Example 15:

Imitative entries by the oboe, English horn, bassoon, French horn, violins, flute, and clarinet (each overlapping somewhat) lead once again to a dynamic *crescendo* with very deliberate accentuation. One final ascending motif in the brass culminates in several heavily-accented chords, bringing the work to a conclusion. A facsimile of the composer's manuscript was printed as a study score by BMI of Canada, Limited. This score is now available from Berandol Music, and should prove most useful for an in-depth study of the music.

VARIATIONS for OBOE, FLUTE, and HARPSICHORD
1965
Harry Freedman

This work is among the compositions that employ some of today's more advanced serial techniques. Reviewing the work when it was recorded by RCA Victor, *The Musical Quarterly* stated: "This is not a neo-Baroque piece, although the instrumentation seems to imply that it is. On the contrary, a twelve-tone theme provides the pitch successions. The variations, each using a different transposition of the row, explore different timbral and textural manipulations. At first, the instruments are interlaced by pairs, then all three share the melodic and rhythmic patterns in a dove-tailed rather than polyphonic manner. Later, more conventional techniques are employed, each instrument playing its own lines in contrapuntal simultaneity. Then there are confrontations of contrasting musical materials: melodic versus rhythmic patterns, lines versus chordal grouping. Solo passages follow canonic treatments, evolve, and so forth. It is an interesting and a very musical piece."

Discussing the **Variations,** which was commissioned by the CBC for the Baroque Trio of Montreal, the composer has written that each variation is "intended to convey some aspect of conversation — dialogue, interruption, argument (both violent and gently persuasive), monologue, badinage, etc. Since at least one person swears that several of the variations remind him of people he actually knows, I should perhaps, have prefaced the work with the usual 'any resemblance to persons living or dead' . . ."

ANALYSIS:

The series on which the ten variations are built is presented by the flute and oboe in duet. The twelve-tone row is:

Example 1:

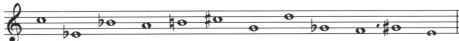

Using this material, the composer builds his basic theme as shown in Example 2.

Example 2:

"Written in 7 meter, the first variation is scored for the same pair of instruments — flute and oboe. This time the original row is transposed up an augmented second (3 semi-tones) as the opening statement is presented.

Example 3: *Variation 1*

Variation 2 continues with the same instrumentation. The meter is simple quadruple and consists basically of a whole note played against a motif of four sixteenth-notes. This configuration is mirrored in each measure between the two instruments, with tones derived from the row.

Example 4: *Variation 2*

Variation 3 introduces the harpsichord as soloist. With tones derived from the row, the variation alternates homophonic and polyphonic styles, ending *pianissimo*.

Example 5: *Variation 3*

Variation 4 requires all three instruments. Written in triple meter, each note is to be played *staccato*. The notes are derived from the original row transposed down one semi-tone. The opening measures are as follows:

Example 6: *Variation 4*

153

Variation 5 begins with a solo flute passage. The notes are derived from the original row but are transposed one semi-tone higher. The meter is compound duple and the two and sometimes three melodies are contrapuntally structured — each line independent. The flute solo commences as follows:

Example 7: *Variation 5*

At the fourth measure, a single-line harpsichord part begins as an accompaniment to the flute. The oboe joins, at the thirteenth measure, in creating three interweaving lines of melody. Gradually the music increases in intensity, ending abruptly.

Variation 6 commences in duple meter, at a fast tempo, with the flute playing the opening series. The tones are derived from the row, only this time the row is transposed up an augmented·fourth.

Example 8: *Variation 6*

With imitative phrases in the flute and oboe lines, the music pulsates forward in contrapuntal style, ending softly on four repeated tones in unison.

Variation 7 should be played fast. There is a continual changing of time signatures, with the beat always remaining an eighth note. The opening measures are chordal in style and are played on the harpsichord, using a series of notes that is the original row transposed up one full·tone.

Example 9: *Variation 7*

Variation 8 is an oboe solo with a short commentary by the harpsichord. The music, in triple meter, is played quite slowly and freely. Commencing on G, the tone row is derived from the original but transposed a fifth higher.

Example 10: *Variation 8*

Variation 9 uses the tone colour of the flute and harpsichord. Commencing slowly, the flute announces the theme which is derived from the row, beginning on the third note Bb in the series. This is transposed up a perfect fourth and therefore commences on Eb. Accompanied at the second measure with the base line of the harpsichord, the two independent lines progress as follows:

Example 11: *Variation 9*

A short flute episode leads to the final phrases which are derived from the opening series in retrograde.

Example 12:

Variation 10 — the last variation — commences with the oboe playing a theme derived from the row. This series is obtained through a transposition of the original up an augmented fifth. The theme commences as follows.

Example 13: *Variation 10*

After a short twelve-measure oboe solo, the flute makes its entry with an independent melodic line. The music continues in duple meter until the harpsichord entry. At this point, the meter changes to quadruple and the texture is chordal, acting as an accompaniment to the flute, and then to the oboe. Becoming more brilliant, the music gathers momentum as it pushes ahead to the last few measures, where it changes dynamically from *fortissimo* to *pianissimo,* finally ending on a five-tone fragment played loudly by the three instruments.

TANGENTS
Symphonic Variations
1967
Harry Freedman

Tangents was commissioned by the National Youth Orchestra Association of Canada under a grant from the Centennial Commission, for premiere performance during Canada's Centennial year, 1967. Discussing his work, Harry Freedman is quoted as saying: "Even though it was commissioned by the National Youth Orchestra, and I did think about the capabilities of its youthful members, there was no great restriction because most of them are just about ready to become professionals. Being young, they were more receptive to new styles."

The composer has further described the music and the compositional techniques he employed in composing **Tangents**: "**Tangents** is a set of variations. The variations are not based on a recognizable theme but on two separate series — the first, a series of 12 notes (12-tone row) and the second, numerical groupings based on the numbers 2 and 3 (3, 2-3, 2, 2-3, 3, 2, 2, 3). The row of 12 notes is used only to determine the choice and sequence of tones. Every other factor in the composition was determined by the numerical series. The variations are not complete entities in themselves, but are continuous. They are grouped (according to mood, tempo, etc.) into three different movements which are played without interruption."

The one-movement work requires approximately fourteen minutes to play. It is scored for the usual-sized orchestra and also includes the harp, glockenspiel, and vibraphone. The musical textures produced by the composer make it a score of unusual subtlety and sophistication — a score that reveals the composer's complete authority and musical artistry. Explanation of the complicated musical structure of the work may prove onerous and time-consuming for the classroom. In its place, specific instrumentation will be discussed to assist and enable the listener to be more discriminatory. The examples given may serve as 'sign-posts' pointing the way as the music progresses.

ANALYSIS:

The work opens with muted strings playing repeated eighth-notes on the tone A.

Example 1:

Against this background, the glockenspiel announces the twelve tones of the row.

Example 2:

Immediately the harp and vibraphone join with the glockenspiel in a second announcement of the row — slightly modified in pitch and rhythm. These notes are presented by the flute at measure 15, accompanied by a thickening of the string texture; for example, the first violins double on the flute, playing *pizzicato*. A new figure is introduced in the trumpets, accompanied by percussion and strings.

Example 3:

This 5-note rhythmic pattern is heard again as it is tossed from one section to another. The strings then continue the pattern at a faster tempo, before relinquishing the motif to the woodwinds.

Example 4:

Half-tone trills may then be heard in all strings — played *pianissimo*.

Example 5:

Beginning at page 19 in the score, the woodwinds (clarinet and bass clarinet) play very softly but at a faster tempo.

Example 6:

Percussion and strings are added to the texture — still *pianissimo*. This figuration is inverted and developed as the delicate orchestration continues. Eventually the tempo changes to very slow (quarter-note = 48). The vibraphone is accompanied by the harp, *pizzicato* violas, and cellos — still scored *piano* and *pianissimo*. This leads into several measures for the strings, where multi-coloured sounds are produced through a multi-division of parts (a most unusual and musically significant passage).

A five-part string section begins at page 33 in the score.

Example 7:

A trio of clarinets overlap and continue; a short harp passage and an ascending string figure signal the return of the full orchestra, which rapidly builds up to a *fortissimo* climax. After a momentary pause, the first and second violins play together in unison, accompanied by brass. Notice the dynamics and the descending direction of the theme.

Example 8:

The vibraphone, glockenspiel, and harp may be heard, with the music gradually becoming slower and softer. A change in tempo to *Allegro* produces unusually delicate sounds with the same instrumentation. Commencing *pianissimo* at page 52, the muted strings accompany a woodwind ensemble. The dynamic intensity increases gradually until a *fortissimo* is reached. An abrupt change to *pianissimo* announces a new motif in the strings.

Example 9:

A woodwind motif is developed above a long sustained chord in the strings. At page 65, a new variation begins with this figure:

Example 10:

Notice the gradually increasing tempo throughout this variation. The music gathers momentum, building toward a point of climax, with a considerable amount of change in the rhythmic elements. A busy percussion section assists in this regard. Several measures before the end, the music becomes more deliberate, with *staccato* and *pizzicato* chording. A slow brass *glissando* brings the music to an abrupt halt — to be followed by a Webernesque echo — and another pause. Immediately, the full orchestra plays a short but very forceful four measures. One final burst from the percussion leads dramatically to the last loud *staccato* chord, bringing the variations to a most satisfying conclusion.

THE WIND AND THE RAIN
Twelfth-Night Epilogue
1974
Harry Freedman

Harry Freedman is a most versatile composer. Although the bulk of his music is instrumental, he has written a number of vocal pieces. His **Keewaydin** for SSA voices is an example. A recent set, entitled **Songs from Shakespeare** for mixed voices (SATB), was written for various stage productions in Ontario. The seven settings are quite suitable for a high school chorus, as technical difficulties are kept to a minimum. The style is reasonably familiar and the experience gained in rehearsing selections from the set should prove stimulating and entertaining.

Published by the composer under the name **Anerca Music,** the last of the series entitled **The Wind and the Rain** is included here for possible use in the classroom. The combined experience of listening to and performing a composer's work should stimulate an ever-increasing interest in the composer and his music.

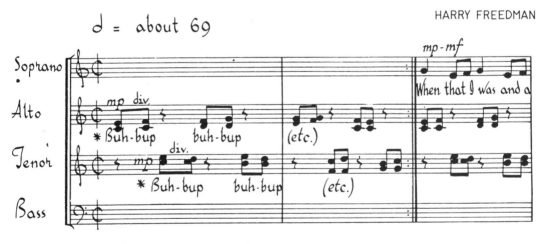

The Wind and the Rain

(TWELFTH NIGHT — EPILOGUE)

HARRY FREEDMAN

♩ = about 69

* Soft b. This applies to t's, d's, and p's in similar articulations throughout the piece. It does not apply to the text.

RALLENTANDO....

diminuendo

.... A .... ♩ = about 60

hey and a ho, the wind and the rain, With swag-g'ring could I ne-ver thrive, for the

hey, ho, wind, rain, da da da da da

RALLENTANDO...A... ♩ = about 100

rain it rain-eth e-v'ry day, but when

rain it rain-eth e-v'ry day.

When I

rain rain rain it rain-eth e-v'ry day, but when

But when I came un-

came bed and the wind

came wind and rain wind

to my bed and rain and the

to my beds, with a hey and a ho, the wind and the rain, with toss pots still had

164

VERY FREE, OUT OF TEMPO
♩ = about 84

fading away . . . .

bup

bup

mf (spoken)

the wind

ssh

and the rain.

and the rain.

and the rain.

and the rain.

*tongue clucks - various high pitches - softly, but as rapidly as possible.

PIERRE MERCURE
1927-1966
Composer and Television Producer

This gifted composer began his creative career in his native city, Montreal, completing his academic studies with Claude Champagne at the Conservatoire de Musique. Born February 21, 1927, his life was tragically cut short through an automobile accident in France on January 27, 1966. Not only was his untimely death a tragedy for his wife and young family, but on that day Canada lost one of its most creative and brilliant musicians — a man whose artistic temperament and musical potential placed him at the centre of Canada's younger generation of composers. Described in the CBC International Service series of Canadian composers' biographies as "one of the most ardent devotees of the avant-garde movement in Canada's musical life," Pierre Mercure was, until his death, in the front rank of contemporary Canadian composers.

At an early age Pierre Mercure received piano instruction from his mother and aunt. He later became a student at the Conservatoire in Montreal where he studied counterpoint and fugue, and a variety of orchestral instruments. Under the guidance of Claude Champagne, with whom he studied harmony and composition, he very early demonstrated his creative talents, producing a variety of songs, theatrical and symphonic music. Encouraged to continue his compositional studies, he travelled to Paris in 1949 to study with Nadia Boulanger, the famous French pedagogue. His association with Boulanger did not last many months, as he preferred to work independently and in collaboration with some of his Quebec colleagues. However, while in Paris he did study orchestration with Arthur Hoéreé, and conducting with Jean Fournet.

On his return to Canada in 1950, Mercure resumed his position as bassoonist with the Montreal Symphony Orchestra. A scholarship from the Quebec government enabled him to further his studies at Tanglewood with Luigi Dallapiccola (serial technique), and electronic music with the Cage-oriented composer, Richard Maxfield. Throughout these early years, and during the early nineteen-fifties in particular, Mercure was pre-occupied with the possibilities of an integration of various art forms. His interests were not confined only to music, but were extended to include creative dance, theatre, and painting. Important works that resulted from these broader influences were: **Ils ont détruit la ville** which, incidentally, won him first prize in a CBC song competition, **Dissidence** — *1955,* for voice and piano; and **Cantate pour une joie** — *1955,* for choir and orchestra.

Early in 1952 Mercure joined the CBC French television network to become its first producer of TV music programmes. As a television producer, he was responsible for a number of artistic productions. He originated and produced the CBC French TV series "L'heure du Concert," including productions of **Orphée, La Bohème, Wozzeck, Oedipus Rex,** and **Pelléas et Mélisande.** His earlier orchestral experience gave him an understanding and appreciation for the many complexities affecting practical performance and communication with an audience. This resulted in a high quality and standard of production which was recognized by his contemporaries. His introduction to and continuous involvement with television made him one of the first Canadian composers to understand in depth the potential and implications of modern media and technology.

Commencing with his incidental music **Alice in Wonderland** (written when the composer was twenty), a number of compositions written in a contemporary vein emerged during the remaining years of Mercure's life. **Kaléidoscope** — *1948,* for medium sized orchestra, was published by Ricordi and recorded by the CBC in the same year under Eric Wild. A recording of this work, played by the Atlantic Symphony Orchestra, is now available and included in the CBC *Canadian Collection.* This important early work was followed by several compositions of unusual significance and musical merit: **Pantomime** — *1949,* is a ballet suite, and was recorded by the CBC International Service under Geoffrey Waddington. Scored for wind, brass, and percussion instruments, it is a work which reflects the influence and appreciation of choreography and the visual arts. **Cantate pour une joie** — *1955,* was also recorded by the CBC International Service. This work again reflects the composer's fascination with the human voice and is, in fact, a composition in which earlier songs from previous works were incorporated into seven movements for soprano voice, choir, and orchestra. **Divertissement** for string quartet and string orchestra followed in 1957. Commissioned by the Lapitsky Foundation, the work was recorded by the CBC under the baton of Alexander Brott, the conductor of the McGill Chamber Orchestra. **Triptyque** for full orchestra was written in 1959. Commissioned by the Vancouver International Festival, it was later published by Ricordi and recorded by the CBC. The availability of Columbia and Odyssey labels has enabled the public to secure recordings of this fine work which won first prize at an International Composers' Competition at Cava dei Tirreni, Italy.

Mercure's music of the early 'sixties demonstrated his growing absorption with electronic media. Although he is numbered among the pioneers of electronic music in Canada, he never produced a pure laboratory electronic work. His tapes are all intended to be played with live performances of various kinds. Examples of such creations would include **Répercussions** — *1961*, for three channels of Japanese carillon sound on magnetic tape; **Tétrachromie**, for three woodwinds, percussion and electronic tape — *1963*. This latter work was released on Columbia records ML-6163 and MS-6763 (scored for ballet), as No. 4 in the CAPAC series of Canadian compositions. Michael Grobin discusses this recording in his survey, "Our Composers on Microgroove — Part II," published in *Musicanada*, March 1970. He writes: "Of his commercially recorded works, the ballet **Tétrachromie** — *1963* satisfied me the most: in ten minutes, and with a single thematic motif for pivot, he conjures up an amazing variety of tonal riches. It takes a fine craftsman to blend electronic tape with woodwinds and treble percussion, using set passages and improvisation . . ." In the following year (1964) Mercure produced **Lignes et points** for orchestra, also recorded by the CBC and RCA Victor. In this work the orchestra is required to simulate electronic effects. Basically a set of variations, the work attempts to suggest geometric figures. It is hoped the CBC will once again release a recording and make it available in the *Canadian Collection*.

Psaume pour abri — *1963*, is another example that demonstrates Mercure's search for unusual sonorities. In the form of a cantata, the work (scored for narrator, two choirs, brass quintet, string quartet, harpsichord, piano, harp, percussion and electronic tape), was an attempt to fuse electronic media with traditional music. Performed initially under the baton of the composer, the music deserves wider exposure through repeated performances. Udo Kasemets in an early discussion of the cantata wrote: ". . . his **Psaume pour abri** (to poems by Fernand Ouellette) remains a sounding testament of a man who once stated that 'to shut our eyes to the phenomenon of change in our lives means to exit from life altogether'."

Two film scores, written in 1965 complete the more than two dozen works composed by Mercure during the twenty years of his creative adult life. Not all were major compositions. However, a high percentage of his pieces are now being heard more frequently on radio, and a considerable number are recorded on CBC and commercial labels. In an assessment of Mercure and his music, Kasemets observed: "Mercure had a musician's ear, a visual artist's eye and a television producer's understanding of movement. He believed in what Emerson had observed a century before him that the laws of each art are convertible into the laws of every other. He treated musical timbres in the manner a painter handles colours, and regarded sound and sound complexes in space as equivalent of lines and planes on canvas."

Predicting the future of a young composer may lead to acute embarrassment. This is not so with Pierre Mercure. The fact that in recent years his music has been given many public performances and is meeting greater public acceptance says much. Had the composer lived longer there is little doubt that he would have become a major influence in Canada. A realization of the worth of his music can only come about with further exposure. For our purposes three pieces which represent his creative output have been selected for detailed listening. **Triptyque, Divertissement,** and **Cantate pour une joie,** are each quite different in their form, and should serve as a useful introduction to the composer's music.

REFERENCES

Davidson, Hugh. "Pierre Mercure 1927-1966."
    Closed Circuit (February 14, 1966).

Desautels, Andrée. "Pierre Mercure." Aspects of Music in Canada
    (Arnold Walter, editor), Toronto:
    University of Toronto Press (1969), pp. 132-133.

Grobin, Michael S. "Our Composers on Microgroove — Part II."
    Musicanada, No. 27 (March, 1970), p. 10.

Kasemets, Udo. "Pierre Mercure." The Music Scene,
    No. 246 (March-April, 1969), pp. 53-56.

"Pierre Mercure." Compositores de América/
    Composers of the Americas, Vol. 5 (1959), pp. 53-56.

"Pierre Mercure." Thirty-four Biographies of Canadian Composers.
    Montreal: CBC International Service (1964), pp. 62-65;
    Reprint, St. Clair Shores, Michigan: Scholarly Press, 1972.

Richer-Lortie, Lyse. "Pierre Mercure." Contemporary Canadian
    Composers (Keith MacMillan and John Beckwith, editors),
    Toronto: Oxford University Press (1975), pp. 152-155.

"A Tribute to Pierre Mercure." The Canadian Composer/
    Le Compositeur Canadien, No. 14 (January, 1967), pp. 10-11.

DIVERTISSEMENT
1957
Pierre Mercure

Mercure's **Divertissement,** for String Quartet and String Orchestra, was given its first performance by the McGill Chamber Orchestra under Alexander Brott. The first movement, indeed the entire work, is in the style of a Concerto Grosso. The second movement is slow and ecstatic, and the closing *Rondo* is dance-like, featuring soloists and orchestra in dialogue.

ANALYSIS:

Movement I *Andante—Allegro*
The slow introductory measures are first announced by the string orchestra. Commencing with the cellos, a rising six-note figure is passed successively on to each of the string parts, thickening the texture as it progresses until the first violins reach their zenith. At this point, the procedure is reversed with a descending line returning to the cellos and basses.

Example 1:

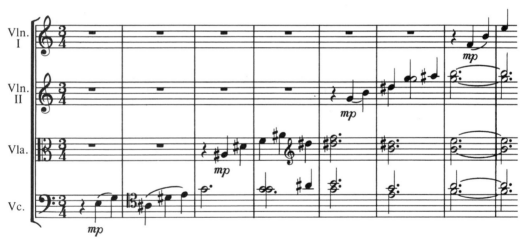

One brief imitative appearance on the solo viola, against shimmering strings, completes the introductory material in readiness for the *Allegro*.

Both the quartet and the string orchestra play the opening measures of the *Allegro* together. In the key of E minor, and with a pulsating triple rhythm, the mood is bright and cheerful. At the ninth measure, the solo violin and solo viola play the theme in octaves against a *pizzicato* accompaniment.

Example 2:

This vigorous theme (now a third lower) is immediately tossed to the unison violins and violas in the orchestra. Another rising melody emerges in the quartet. It is heard at first on the viola, and later it is passed to the violins, and again to the remainder of the orchestra.

Example 3:

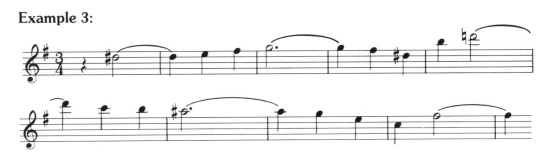

With alternating episodes, the thematic material passes to each of the instrumental forces in musical dialogue, creating a balance between melodic and rhythmic interest.

Movement II *Adagio*
This is a very interesting little movement of only 50 measures duration. In the key of D minor, it begins very slowly and softly, and gradually builds toward a climax at the mid-point. From there onwards the music is mirrored (played retrograde), coming to a quiet, gentle conclusion, as it began.

Two *pianissimo* chords precede the rising motif.

174

Example 4:

The undulating contours continue, leading into a rising *pizzicato* in simple triple rhythm in the string orchestra. Opposing this theme, the string quartet plays a descending theme in a compound triple rhythm.

Example 5:

Thus we hear cross-rhythms and opposing directional melodic lines simultaneously — but only for a few measures, before the mid-point is reached and the entire process is reversed.

This movement, because of its relative simplicity, provides an excellent example for the study of mirroring as a modern technical device employed by contemporary composers.

Movement III *Rondo Presto*

Again in the key of E minor, and in $\frac{6}{8}$ meter throughout, the characteristically rising melodic lines are present. Eight measures of introduction precede the main theme which is announced first in the solo viola line, and then in succeeding quartet parts.

Example 6:

Alternating *leggiero* and *marcato* treatments between quartet and orchestra create musical interest as the thematic elements are developed and stated in each of the opposing forces. Later in the score, the violas (and still later the first violins) play the theme in dialogue.

Example 7:

Further repetition of the main theme (Example 6) occurs as the spirited movement reaches its climax at the last few measures of the score, completing the cycle of thematic repetitions one expects in a rondo.

176

TRIPTYQUE
1959
Pierre Mercure

This work was composed as the result of a commission from the Vancouver International Festival in 1959. It later won the composer first prize at the Fourth International Composers' Competition at Cava dei Tirreni, Italy. The work may possibly become one of the compositions by which the composer is best remembered.

As suggested by the title, the music is in three movements; a short *Adagio,* an *Allegro,* and the final *Adagio* which is the first movement played backwards. Both the first and third movements are slow and quiet, so the composer obtains contrast by building the central movement on a theme of 'bouncing velocity and gale force.'

ANALYSIS:

Movement I *Adagio*
Beginning very softly, the cellos and string basses announce the ascending theme. The remaining strings also assist in the rising and falling contour of the opening measures.

Example 1:

A three-measure solo on the oboe immediately follows the introduction.

Example 2:

This is followed by an answering phrase on the flute.

Example 3:

Short motifs in the woodwinds and brass, over a softly shimmering string accompaniment, bring the short *Adagio* to a close.

Movement II *Allegro marcato*

This movement is written in ternary form. A three-measure rhythmic pattern on the snare drum serves as an introduction to the movement. Repeated immediately, the tempo of the movement is established with this lively rhythm.

Example 4:

Joined by the full orchestra, the music is propelled forward by a strongly syncopated figure, while the strings, brass, and woodwinds pursue ascending melodic patterns that quickly grow in intensity.

A new unison string pattern emerges from the first example.

Example 5:

Here the rhythmic accent returns to the first two beats in each measure as the orchestra rushes head-long in another burst of fury. Momentary respite occurs with short ascending phrases in the woodwinds. Triplet figures are employed as the texture becomes more transparent.

Example 6:

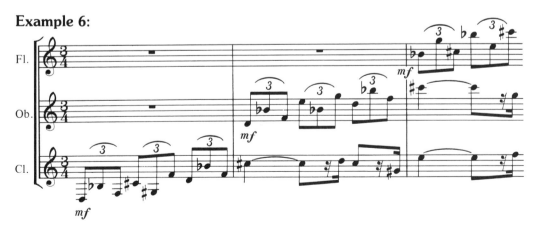

With short fragmentary motifs set against the vigorous percussion section, the music continues with wide dynamic fluctuations. After a relatively quiet section which is played predominantly by the winds, the mood again becomes more aggressive. This occurs through the recapitulation of the exposition. Although not a strict repetition of the earlier material, the basic rhythms are preserved together with the same dynamic elements, and the same relentless speed.

Movement III *Adagio*
This movement is identical to the first movement, except that it is written in retrograde form. Therefore the last chord of movement I becomes the first chord in movement III. This 'repliement' structure produces some interesting sounds — particularly with the short woodwind solo phrases that, of course, are played retrograde also.

Example 7:

Whereas the opening statement of the first movement has an ascending contour, the last few measures of the work are in reverse, producing a descending line, which concludes the work on a peaceful *pianissimo* chord. Both the first and third movements would serve as a useful comparison for the listener. Because of their structural simplicity and their brevity, the two movements serve to illustrate the contemporary compositional technique of mirroring thematic elements.

CANTATE POUR UNE JOIE
1955
Pierre Mercure

The text of this cantata, for soprano solo, choir, and orchestra, was written by Mercure's life-long friend Gabriel Charpentier, himself a composer and producer at the CBC. Mercure had earlier set poems by Charpentier to music, and at his friends' urging, used the seven sections of the text as a basis for his 'Cantata for a Joy'. The respective sections of the text are entitled:

> The Young Lions; Psalm; They Have Destroyed the Village;
> Lament; Black Pierrot; Chorale; A Cry of Joy.

Written originally in French by Charpentier, the English version was translated by Harold Heiberg. Two versions are now available, one with an orchestral accompaniment, and the other with a piano reduction by Ruggero Vene.

In a short discussion of the work, Udo Kasemets wrote: . . . "its seven sections create a vivid almost surrealistic picture borne from the agony of our time. Mercure's musical speech is here extremely direct and simple. The dissonant harmonies are handled with vocal smoothness, the orchestral accompaniment is picturesque and the voices, including the solo part, are kept in a comfortable range."

ANALYSIS:

I. The Young Lions

> naked terror stalks the village
> in the desert roar the yellow lions
> and the dark shadows surround my dwelling
> fear is all we know
> the fire licks at the foot of the mountain
> ah! that the men and the women all would perish
> that the flowers and the birds all would die

ah! close your eyes, your shining eyes
and save your most highly prized possessions
the brave young men are all dead
oh! hear the weeping maidens mourn
with words that are not their own
now all is lost and crying for vengeance is futile
caught in a trap is indignation
Lord, Thy servant low is laid and crushed is my spirit
to Thee I cry, in mercy look on me
fear is all we know
hungry flames lick at the hill
naked fear stalks through the village
and the young lions roar in the desert

A short instrumental introduction consisting of six measures of *molto lento* followed by a short *vivo e incisivo* precedes the SATB chorus singing, 'in the desert roar the yellow lions'. The statement in the key of F-sharp minor is presented as follows.

Example 1:

This chant-like introduction is immediately followed by the soprano soloist with, 'the fire licks at the foot of the mountain'.

Example 2:

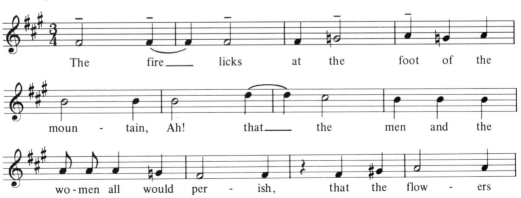

Although written in triple time, there is a flexibility in the vocal lines that strongly suggest (through the accentuation) duple rhythms. With the mixed chorus accompanying the soloist, the dialogue continues in similar style, with the emphasis alternating at times between soloist and chorus. Repetition of the phrase also occurs in the tenor and bass lines.

Example 3:

The gradual build-up of tonal forces gently subsides as the chorus and soloist repeat very quietly the phrase, 'and the young lion roars in the desert', bringing the short movement to a close.

II. Psalm *Piuttòsto lento*

deep disgust for things too heavily perfumed and facile —
    brings in its wake a raging storm which shall be our doom.
in the darkened sky gleams a single star through the gloom —
    this star will lead me onward into joy.
here in my humble abode, long forlorn and empty —
    now at last I dwell no more alone
I hear his breathing close beside me —
    and the sound is soothing to my soul.
now there is a hand wherein I may place my hand
    in smiling confidence and trust unswerving.
now harmonies awake and sing —
    where music was heard no more.
I trudge exhaustedly on the cobbles of the roadway —
    I fall and bloody both my aching knees.
O friend of all my days never leave me I implore —
    for alone I am lost
all at once in the night which long had known my tears —
    the tears I shed for all mankind.
all at once, he is here in the night, beside me close —
    to guide me from the dark into light.

A six-measure introduction precedes the soprano entry on the words, 'deep disgust for things too heavily perfumed and facile brings in its wake a raging storm which shall be our doom.'

Example 4:

In a similar declamatory style, and without change of key, the movement progresses quietly, yet with a certain tranquility, as it alternately presents soloists and accompanying chorus. An almost chant-like quality in the four-part vocal texture provides a suitable mood to the words: 'here in my humble abode, at last I dwell no more alone!'

Example 5:

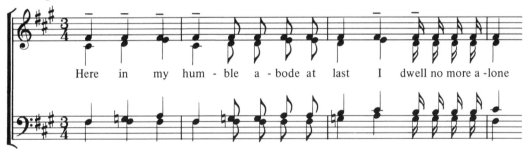

Throughout the entire movement there is a smoothness of vocal line that perfectly matches the mood and expression of the text and the unobtrusive accompaniment.

III. They Have Destroyed the Village *Molto lento*

> they have destroyed the village
> drowned are the rocks and the rats the men and women
> in the fire are laughter and wild Norman dances
> circling the flames in a round dance and a sarabande
> laughter cries and raucous shouts leather the boots
> ancient houses and more ancient roads are ruined
> rocks overrun by rodents and rats
> stunned men stand dumb with horror
> pregnant women are weeping

The four-measure orchestral introduction is identical to the opening statement in part one. This leads into the choir announcement, 'they have destroyed the city.'

Example 6:

One measure of accompaniment leads into the solo statement, 'drowned are the rocks and the rats the men and the women in the fire are laughter and wild Norman dances'.

Example 7:

Here in the third section there is a noticeable change in the vocal lines with a wider range of intervals employed. The work becomes more dramatic and intense in both vocal and orchestral textures illustrating the poignancy of the text.

IV. Lament *Andante molto*

in my saddened spirit	alas I cannot I cannot	I long for the night
my city expires	yet filled with yearning	when I shall be entombed
could I but be borne away	I find myself a clown	in dust
and sunk into a quagmire	Pierrot with no moonlight	on rutted roadway
ah thus I could rejoin	in the darkness all the day	where escape is forbidden
all my comrades long dead	to behold light no more	ah I long for this joy

184

This short section is scored for soprano soloist and solo strings. Sung in a recitative style in compound quadruple time, the opening line, 'in my saddened spirit my city expires,' is presented as follows.

Example 8:

In my sad - dened spi - rit___ my cit - y ex - pires___

V. Black Pierrot *Vivo e leggiero*

> black Pierrot, Harlequin yellow
> to the guitar are dancing on carpet white
> white as the sombre face of Pierrot
> on crimson carpet billowing sleeves
> are filled by the breeze
> head slightly tilted eyes smiling sadly
> high on the stage above entrechat
> Harlequin has stolen a guitar
> the nameless ballerina hangs suspended
> harpsichord a-tinkling out of tune
> down the street of night
> where black Pierrot his long sleeves is trailing
> comes running the guitar of Harlequin the yellow
> and twangs on a string it has broken

A seven-measure introduction in triple time prefaces the four-part chorus. Bright and lively throughout, the short section offers a welcome contrast to the previous sombre music.

Example 9:

Very dance-like in character, the music admirably suits the text although it concludes almost too soon.

VI. Chorale *Moderato e accentuato*

> marching marching endlessly on
> my spirit must abandon reluctantly
> the death of far too happy dreams
> its cry came from afar through melancholy shadows
> and its body now made clean
> purified by mists infernal
> has slowly disappeared from view
> beyond the pale mirages

A short three-measure introduction announces the chorus singing, 'marching, marching endlessly on.'

Example 10:

Moving between triple and quadruple rhythms, the chorus is joined once again by the soprano soloist; but only for a few measures, for like the previous section, the music is extremely short.

VII. A Cry of Joy *Presto*

> a cry of joy has escaped from my body
> everywhere I look are people dancing
> among the columns inverted
> my cry of joy moves on ahead of me
> I shall follow its call
> its light will fill my path with glory
> and all of its commands I shall obey
> the young man has departed beyond the sea
> bearing with him the sheaves of gladiolus blooms
> and his cry is one of gladness

Ten measures of introduction in the key of D major set the mood for 'a cry of joy', which is sung by the soprano.

Example 11:

Later the tenors and basses sing in unison.

Example 12:

The mixed choir continues, aided by short commentaries from the soprano soloist. The writing then becomes more polyphonic as each part begins with the words, 'a cry of joy has escaped from my body.'

With a gradual build-up of both orchestral and vocal forces, the music soars to a climactic point, culminating in a joyful ending on the words, 'his cry is one of gladness, is one of gladness.'

Pierre Mercure was a young man of under thirty years of age when he wrote this work. His compositions had already begun to show his tremendous creative potential. The music that he wrote during the following decade fully demonstrates the power of musical invention that he possessed, and that was so tragically short-lived. The three works chosen for analytical listening should provide in some measure further insight, and help create a greater awareness of his musical artistry.

R. MURRAY SCHAFER
1933
Composer, Author, Educator

Of all the composers living in Canada today, none has experienced such a meteoric rise to fame as has Murray Schafer. He was relatively unknown even a decade ago, but today he is without question one of Canada's most successful composers. His fame and reputation are world-wide, for he is known internationally as an author, composer, music educator, speaker, and researcher of the world sound-environment. Such a phenomenal rise to prominence is probably without precedence in Canadian musical life, for barely five years ago any discussion of Schafer's musical stature would likely have proved to be rather provocative and controversial — particularly among his contemporaries. Suzanne Ball, a free-lance writer, reinforces this view-point in her opening statement on Schafer in the May-June, 1970 issue of *The Music Scene:* "Murray Schafer is like religion and politics . . . you don't argue about him in polite company. You're either very much for him or very much against him, and if you belong in the latter category chances are you won't see 50 again." Here, in the mid-seventies, it is quite apparent that Murray Schafer possesses the ability to function in several capacities, and his tremendous success in each endeavour has done much to allay any, if not all misgivings of the unconverted.

Born in Sarnia, Ontario, July 18, 1933, Murray commenced piano lessons at the age of six. Although he did not particularly like the instrument, he continued his studies, ultimately graduating with an LRSM (Licentiate of the Royal Schools of Music, London, England). Although Schafer describes his formal education as 'dog-eared,' he did study piano with Alberto Guerrero and theory and composition with John Weinzweig, both at the Royal Conservatory of Music, Toronto. Still later, in 1958, he continued studies in England with Peter Racine Fricker. His disenchantment with high school (he is quoted by Peter Such as saying, 'high school was a revolting experience'), and later with the University of Toronto, was certainly not an impediment to his education, for in later years, on his own, he studied counterpoint, Latin, German, French, Italian, and Arabic. He read widely in philosophy and literature, and today these influences and interests are readily discernible in his music.

Murray Schafer's career has been varied. After his initial encounter with the 'establishment,' he left Toronto in 1956 for Europe. During the next five years, he lived in Vienna and later in England, working as a free-lance writer in radio and music journalism. For the young composer, this was a period in which his musical experience was broadened and enriched. His discussions and correspondence with Ezra Pound and his association with the BBC resulted in interviews with musicians and composers as well as musical travelogues. His books, *British Composers in Interview,* and his editing of Pound's complete musical writings for the American publisher, Prentice-Hall, Inc., were written as a direct result of this interest. The latter book, subsequently translated and published in French and German, also resulted in an authoritative article on Ezra Pound appearing in the Summer, 1961 issue of *The Canadian Music Journal.*

Shortly after his visit with Pound, Murray Schafer and a former Toronto music student, Phyllis Mailing, were married in London, England. Returning to Canada in 1961, they settled for a short time in Toronto. Among his activities was the founding of Ten Centuries Concerts, of which he became the first president. This organization was a collaborative effort designed to promote new and rarely heard music. During this period, Schafer's own important works were: **Concerto for Harpsichord and Eight Wind Instruments**—*1954*; **Minnelieder**—*1956*, for soprano and instrumental ensemble; **In Memoriam: Alberto Guerrero**—*1959*, for string orchestra; **Protest and Incarceration**—*1960*; and **Canzoni for Prisoners**—*1962*. These works reveal a rapid development over an eight-year period. Andree Desautels, in *Aspects of Music in Canada*, expresses the nature of this development and traces the evolution of style and change from polytonality, through pantonality, to atonality. Certainly the latter two compositions indicate the direction his later works would take. His concern for the culture of the times, for man's inhumanity to man, and the unjust society in which we live become more evident in the works immediately following.

In 1963, Murray Schafer accepted an invitation to become artist-in-residence at Memorial University in St. John's, Newfoundland. Although he had no actual commitment to teaching, he did, in fact, have some contact with students interested in music. Opportunities for working with music students in Toronto during the summer of 1964 also gave him access to the classroom, resulting in the publication, *Composer in the Classroom*—1965. Three other booklets entitled *Ear Cleaning*—1967; *The New Soundscape*—1969; and *When Words Sing*—1970; followed in rapid succession. These useful educational resources, published by Berandol Music, have been written as a result of the composer's ever-growing interest in sound and in music education, and in his increasing concern with the effects of noise pollution. Since his appointment to the Communication Centre at Simon Fraser University, Burnaby, Vancouver in 1965, the composer has written extensively on various aspects of music education. He does not provide methods or classroom routines, but instead acts as a catalyst, provoking, inspiring, and expanding his students' sensory awareness of the musical environment. His many articles, published in a variety of national and international journals, all contribute to his stature as a composer who is vitally aware and responsive to the needs of music education. His education theories are also further explained in a National Film Board Documentary entitled *Bing Bang Boom,* which gained first prize in the educational film competition in New York in 1970. Such compositions as his **Statement in Blue**—*1964;* **Threnody**—*1966* (revised 1967); and **Epitaph for Moonlight**—*1968;* were specifically written for school performance and have since proved to be fascinating works for high school study. The scores of these three works, published by Berandol, demonstrate the composer's unusual graphic ability and his originality in developing new notational techniques.

In recent years, several writers have attempted to describe Schafer's music. The published brochure by BMI Canada offers the following observations: "Schafer's music is a peculiar synthesis of twentieth century avant-garde techniques and the spirit of nineteenth century romanticism. Not that there are any echoes in his music of a Schumann or Wagner. To the contrary: the style, texture, and manner of Schafer's music is unmistakably of the second half of the twentieth century. It is the content of Schafer's music that shows the composer's affinity with such thinkers as Nietzsche and Freud. More often than not, his works written on his own texts are sombre and impassioned pronouncements on human and world conditions." A closer look at certain subjects and texts will disclose the content of the composer's enraged comments about social ills and world conditions. For example, there is his now famous **Threnody** which utilizes quotations from burned victims of the Nagasaki nuclear bomb-blast. Here the power of words and the emotional impact of the orchestral and choral forces impart a powerful devastating message to both listener and performer alike. His **Requiems for the Party-Girl**—*1966*, dramatizes the act of suicide of a lonely person; while **Gita**—*1967*, for mixed chorus, brass, and electronic tape, is all about the serenity of spirit and the dangers of egoism and passion. Similarly, his previously-mentioned **Canzoni for Prisoners** reflects the constant violation of human rights and dignity; while **Protest and Incarceration** is a condemnation of dictatorship and injustice.

Udo Kasemets discusses Murray Schafer's music in the recently published *Contemporary Canadian Composers*. He contends that 'much of the composer's source material is of extramusical origin.' An examination of the titles of recent compositions such as **Divan i Shams i Tabriz**—*1969;* **In Search of Zoroaster**—*1971;* and **From the Tibetan Book of the Dead**—*1968;* reveals the strong influence of both European and Eastern philosophy and literature as well as a concentration on mythology, symbolism, and mysticism. The use of texts in Sanskrit, Tibetan, Persian, Egyptian, and Greek, also reflects his understanding of and sensitivity to the impact of language. The sounds of the languages are basically intrinsic to the music and not merely outward adornments. Their programmatic content and musical characteristics create opportunities as vehicles of musical expression for the composer.

In 1970 Professor Schafer published *The Book of Noise.* Research into the acoustical environment led the composer, at that time, to write: "A fascinating macrocosmic symphony is being played ceaselessly around us. It is the symphony of the world soundscape." Subsequent research resulted in his receiving an award of $39,000.00 in 1972 from the Canadian Donner Foundation for a study on sound and its effect on people. This on-going research, entitled *The World Soundscope Project,* is a study of man's relation to sonic environment and has already made its initial impact in both published and recorded material. In addition to such publications as *The Music of the Environment*—1974 (the Vancouver Soundscape), the CBC in October, 1974, began a series of programmes designed to give greater coverage to the part played by Schafer and his colleagues at the Sonic Research Studio, Simon Fraser University. A more detailed report of this project was published in the November-December, 1974 issue of *The Music Scene.* One immediate impact of this initial interest in sound is the composer's **Okeanos**—*1971,* a quadraphonic tape composition exploring sounds and images of the sea.

During the ten years that Murray Schafer has lived in Vancouver, his musical output has been remarkable. Large scale works for the stage, for orchestra, for soloists and orchestra, for choirs, and for a wide variety of instrumental and electronic media have been commissioned, composed, and performed. His opera, **Loving** (Toi)—*1965,* is a bilingual work and was commissioned by the CBC and first performed on the CBC-TV Montreal network under Serge Garant. His **Patria** is a large-scale trilogy intended for performance on three consecutive nights. The first two parts deal with the theme of loneliness — of alienated people living in hostile environments. The second part is better known as **Requiems for the Party-Girl.** Completed in 1972, this work is identified by Schafer as 'musical theatre.' Commenting on the premiere performance, John Kraglund, in the *Globe and Mail* wrote: ". . . As a conglomerate with a strong dramatic appeal, and an ability to grip

192

the spectators' attention with a snake-like fascination, it is brilliant. Whatever one may think of it, there is no doubt that Schafer has again created something that will keep audiences and critics talking until his next production makes an appearance."

Schafer is identified in Canada as a national figure in music, with more than forty major works listed in his catalogue and numerous books and articles on a variety of musical topics. One need only scan the pages of each issue of *The Music Scene* to discover the number of performances of his works in Canada and overseas that occur increasingly year by year. Schafer's ability as a speaker and Canadian representative has taken him to most quarters of the globe. In the last several years, he has undoubtedly become the most travelled musician in Canada. He travelled extensively through Europe during the early months of 1975 on a lecture tour sponsored by Universal Edition.

Still active in his efforts to direct the *World Soundscape Project,* he will continue to assist his colleagues at Simon Fraser in their continuing research of the European soundscape. With so many diverse activities, it is little wonder that Professor Schafer has decided to leave the confines and demands of university life. On his return to Canada in the early summer of 1975, he settled once again in Ontario, living a somewhat secluded life with more freedom to pursue his musical composition. Because of his inherent genius for creating works of art in the literary and compositional field, the world of music will look expectantly toward the future and follow with anticipation the artistic fulfillment of one of Canada's most gifted native sons.

REFERENCES

Ball, Suzanne. "Murray Schafer — Composer, Teacher, and Author."
    The Music Scene, No. 253 (May-June, 1970), pp. 7-8.

"R. Murray Schafer — A Portrait." *Musicanada,* No. 14
    (October, 1968), pp. 8-9.

"R. Murray Schafer." *Compositores de Américas/*
    Composers of the Americas, Vol. 10 (1964), pp. 98-103.

Schafer, R. Murray. "Threnody: A Religious Piece for our Time."
    Music, AGO/RCCO Magazine, Vol. 4, No. 5 (May, 1970), pp. 33-35.

Such, Peter. "R. Murray Schafer." *Soundprints,* Toronto:
    Clarke, Irwin and Company Limited (1972), pp. 126-162.

THRENODY
1966
R. Murray Schafer

Threnody, a song of lamentation, is a work of such power and emotional impact that it may shock many people when it is first heard. It is an anti-war protest that strikes at the stupidity of war. Such a subject is not calculated to disturb people in the normal sense, but the forces unleashed in the performance of the work are of such a nature that the culminating impact is almost overpowering. **Threnody** is a religious piece of our time. Its message cries out against all undignified behavior such as war, racial discrimination, and the violation of human rights. Its message has strong humanistic implications, cutting deeply into man's consciousness.

The composer has described **Threnody** as "an uncomfortable work." Conceived in a contemporary idiom, it is scored for youth orchestra, youth choir, five narrators, and electronic tape. The texts, spoken by the narrators, come from two documents: (1) eye-witness accounts by children and young people of the atomic bombing of Nagasaki on August 9, 1945; and (2) comments and telegrams to and from the Potsdam Conference in July, 1945, after the first successful test explosion by the United States. In performance the first text is spoken by children. The second text is heard on tape, spoken by adult voices.

In a discussion of the work published in the May, 1970 issue of *Music,* the AGO/RCCO journal, the composer describes certain characteristics of **Threnody**. "The music of **Threnody** is in a contemporary idiom, but it is always conceived for the age group for which it was intended. Within a controlled framework there are numerous sections where the young singers and instrumentalists are given opportunities for thoughtful improvisations. 'Thoughtful' rather than spontaneous because the improvisatory sections are always set in apposition to portions of the spoken texts for which they must set an appropriate mood and illumination. In rehearsal, I usually try to have the instrumental soloists and the speakers rehearse together, drawing the musicians' attention constantly to the character of the words they are accompanying. To perform **Threnody** properly, one must take up an ethical position on the subject matter."

In 1967 and 1968, two performances were reviewed by Robert Sunter of the *Vancouver Sun* in most laudatory terms: "**Threnody,** a new composition by Murray Schafer, left most of the 600 people in North Vancouver's Centennial Theatre furtively dabbing their eyes Sunday night . . . From these forces (the performers), Schafer drew some extraordinary sounds which had powerful emotional and dramatic impact . . . Schafer clearly set out to shock — musically, emotionally, verbally. And in this he succeeded without a doubt . . . Emotionally, the work achieved its greatest impact in its finale. After an enormous crescendo of electronic noise

194

that defies description, the tumult gave way to an ethereal wordless postscript by the choir that was like an echo from another world." "Murray Schafer's nuclear aftermath composition, **Threnody,** overshadowed everything else at Friday's Community Concert in Queen Elizabeth Theatre . . . Its performance was both harrowing and compelling. This was the second time I had heard **Threnody** and I can say quite categorically it is the most moving piece of music composed in the last 20 years that I have heard . . . There was no doubt in my mind that the tortured sounds Schafer created, the almost literal representations of bomb blast, searing wind, moaning casualties and mourning, manipulated the emotions of the listeners even more than the descriptions of burnt flesh and shredded skin."

The score of **Threnody** is published by Berandol Music Limited, Toronto. This is emphasized because a study of the music would be enhanced if at least one copy of the music is available in the classroom. The departure from usual notation for certain musical effects is graphically portrayed by Schafer in such a way that only an examination of the full score could suffice for full explanation. The score is a work of art in itself and a study of the notational devices utilized by the composer could prove rewarding.

ANALYSIS:
The work takes approximately seventeen minutes to perform. Because of the many opportunities given to choir and orchestra to improvise, no two performances would be exactly alike. However, the time guide-lines are specific, and within these controls a variety of interpretations is possible. All spoken texts are given with appropriate cues and signals clearly indicated.

Threnody begins with a *staccato* chord played by percussion instruments. A gradual *crescendo* builds with the addition of the brass against a high sustained *tremolo* on strings until, after approximately 25-30 seconds, the first cue is given with the commencement of the electronic tape. During the first half-minute of the tape, the orchestral forces are unleashed; first a *crescendo,* and then a *decrescendo.* A solo piccolo prepares the listeners for the first two speakers. At this point the accompaniment provided is basically improvisatory. After two and a half minutes, the chorus enters dramatically against instrumental accompaniment. With each of the five voices crying out their messages of grief, the music builds and rebuilds tension upon tension — until all is silence. A spoken voice, then a soprano and chorus are interrupted by the tape announcement of a successful bombing mission.

Little by little, the gruesome text is recited against the instrumental accompaniment — always building levels of emotional intensity rarely experienced in orthodox music. An awareness of the devastation produces its emotional impact on both performer and listener alike as the story unfolds. Few scores of our time have the ability to produce such intensity of feeling and expression. Few scores have so eloquently disturbed the emotional facade of listening audiences.

THRENODY

R. Murray Schafer

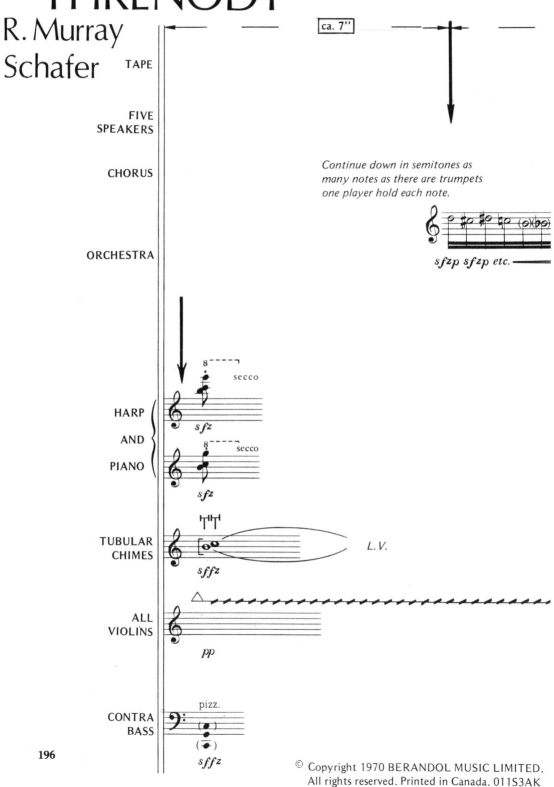

Continue down in semitones as
many notes as there are trumpets
one player hold each note.

sfzp sfzp etc. ———

196

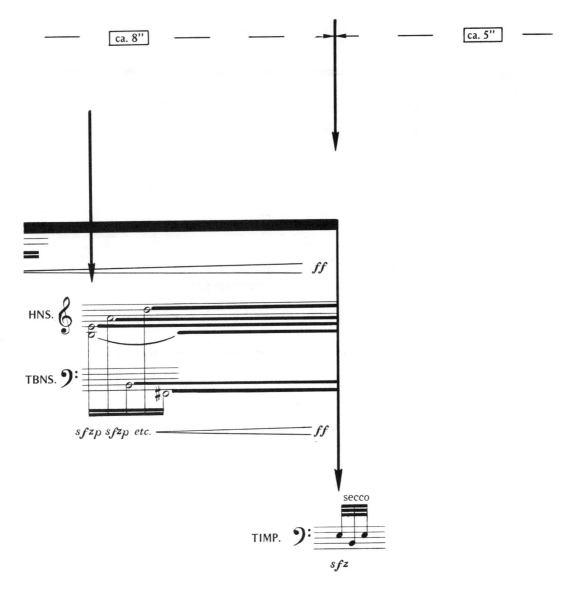

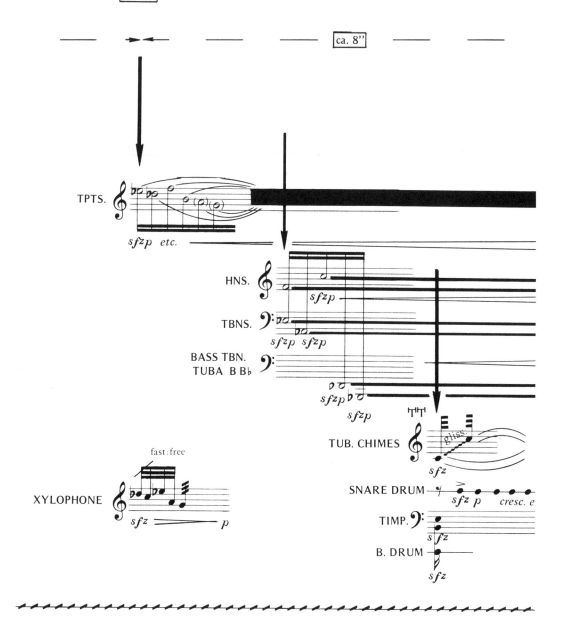

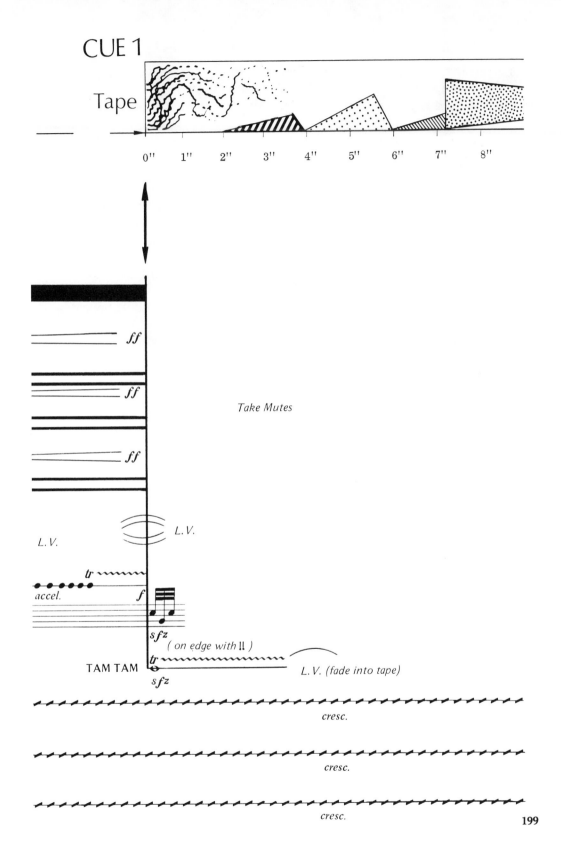

This is music that does not require a 'blow-by-blow' account. To simply know and hear the message it proclaims, and to realize the enormity of man's ability to annihilate mankind is sufficient in itself. The work is, however, a work of art. It is a work that will be heard many times. The composer in his own words has said: "I hope **Threnody** will travel the most, the farthest, and the deepest. I literally want it to be performed to death. I want it to be performed until it is no longer necessary. Then I will burn the score."

Threnody was commissioned by the Alumnae of the Royal Conservatory of Music for the Vancouver Junior Symphony Orchestra. It has been performed a number of times by high school music groups. The recording, obtainable under the Melbourne label, features the Lawrence Park Collegiate Orchestra and Choir with members of the North Toronto Collegiate Orchestra under the direction of John P. Barron and John R. McDougall. It provides a most faithful and sensitive rendition of the score. Schools that possess the musical resources could benefit by the experience of rehearsal and performance of this work.

EPITAPH for MOONLIGHT
1968
R. Murray Schafer

Epitaph for Moonlight is a study-piece for youth choir. It was intended as an ear-training exercise, for the singers must learn to pitch their tones by interval from key tones which are given. As with **Threnody**, the score is written graphically rather than in the usual conventional notation and, like many of the composer's scores, is impressive for its art work as well as its musical ideas.

The notes that accompany the Berandol Music score give certain directions which shed light on Schafer's intentions. "It is understood that while the piece contains few dynamic markings, it is almost always soft. Dynamics are indicated by the thickness of the line. A thin line is a soft sound, a heavy line a loudish one." In his discussion of the text used by the choir, Schafer explains: "I once gave a grade 7 class the assignment of finding suitable synonyms for the word 'moonlight' — new words in a private language were to be invented that expressed in sound the concept of moonlight. The text of the present composition consists of some of these synonyms." A few examples are quoted from the score: Nu-yu-yuh, malooma, shiverglowa, shalowa, sheelesk.

Since the original recording was released on the Melbourne label, the CBC has recorded the work with the Festival Singers of Canada. In 1972, shortly after the Toronto Mendelssohn Choir returned from their first European tour, their conductor, Elmer Iseler, is quoted as saying: "Do you know, every time we did Schafer's work **Epitaph for Moonlight** they broke out in spontaneous applause." Iseler's work with the Festival Singers is internationally recognized. His recording of this work is another example of a beautiful performance by a Canadian choir singing music by a Canadian composer.

ANALYSIS:

The work is scored for youth choir with optional bells, such as glockenspiels, metalophones, vibraphones, and triangles. Beginning on a medium-high note, the sopranos divide into four parts, each descending a semi-tone, always *pianissimo*. Each voice part — alto, tenor, and bass divides similarly, humming for approximately 20 seconds before vocalizing on one of the original words from the text.

The graphic representation is an interesting example of the composer's ability to notate his musical ideas. With a spectrum of sound ranging from high to low, using vowels and whisperings, the score provides opportunities for improvisation. Freedom to sing expressively and in harmony, in the confines of limited dynamics, creates a most attractive conglomerate of sound. With the added attractiveness of delicate bell sounds, the short composition offers a lovely panorama of sensitive sound production. Here is music that is uniquely different from the usual 'school' music. Here is a score which could prove challenging to the imagination, and aid performers and listeners in developing an ear for contemporary musical expression.

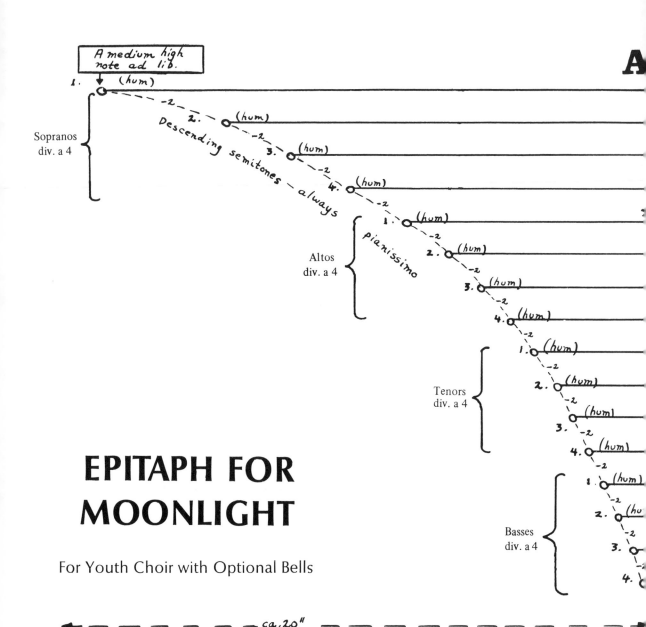

A

A medium high note ad lib.

Sopranos div. a 4

Altos div. a 4

Tenors div. a 4

Basses div. a 4

Descending semitones – always

Pianissimo

ca. 20"

EPITAPH FOR MOONLIGHT

For Youth Choir with Optional Bells

Optional
Glockenspiels,
Metalophones,
Vibraphones,
Triangles,
Small Bells, etc.

STRING QUARTET No. 1
1970
R. Murray Schafer

Murray Schafer's **String Quartet** was commissioned by and dedicated to the Purcell String Quartet, Vancouver. The work was premiered at the Vancouver Art Gallery by the Purcell Quartet during a series of summer concerts in 1970. It is an extremely imaginative work that has few if any peers in its style and complexity. It breaks new ground in its demands upon performer and listener alike, and requires, even demands full attention for its full impact to be felt. Discussing the first performance, a critic for the *Vancouver Sun,* Lloyd Dykk, wrote: "Its impression will be with me for some time. Schafer's **Quartet** is as arresting a piece of music as I've heard in a long while . . . It threatens to shatter the extendable confines afforded by two violins, viola, and cello. Yet it does remain within; it uses the resources of the string quartet in an extremely imaginative way, and, as far as one can surmise from a single listening, it is a viable piece of musical argument."

The composer describes the music as follows: "It is in one movement and is characterized by an intensity throughout. The first several minutes of the quartet are scored for all four players, giving the impression that they are locked together, with each trying unsuccessfully to break away from the others. When they finally break free, a calm solo section follows for first violin. At the middle of the work, a long unison section begins, at first very slowly and quietly but gradually reaching a ferocious intensity and tempo, then suddenly breaking into a series of snapshot flashes of previous material. These snapshots become briefer in duration, but clearer in focus towards the close. Eventually, the 'camera' goes on snapping even though the 'film' has run out — giving a curiously surrealistic close to the composition."

ANALYSIS:
The score of this work, published by Universal Edition (London), demonstrates once again Murray Schafer's originality in his use of notational devices. Bar lines are rarely employed. In their place various time slots are indicated from 0" through to the end at 15'50". These timings are for guidance only — particularly in the early stages of rehearsal.

The music, although in one movement, has three definable stages of fast-slow-fast. Within this design there is flexibility because of the opportunities afforded the group and individual players for spontaneous improvisation. The music commences on middle C in unison and immediately each part struggles to move away from each other, through 32nd note figurations and glissandos. The effect is one of being 'locked together' — each attempting to disengage himself. Here is a reproduction of the opening statement.

Example 1:

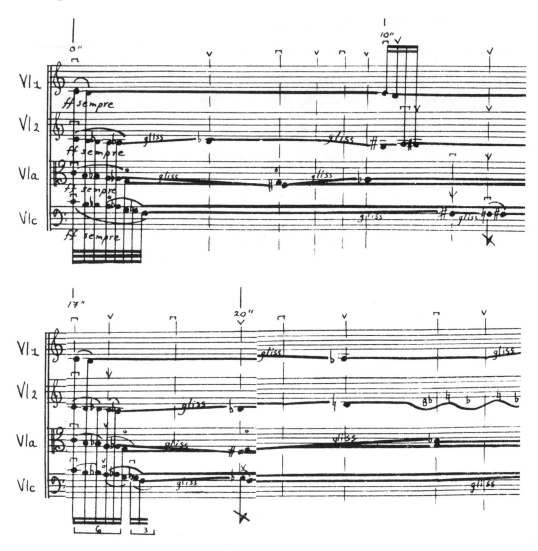

Immediately one notices the aural intensity of the music, as dynamic levels alternate wildly and as the tempo changes veer somewhat erratically in either direction. Various bowing techniques and *pizzicato* are employed as the music of this first section progresses. The second violin succeeds in 'breaking away' after approximately four minutes, rushing onwards in an ascending direction. But only momentarily — for the first violin commences with an expressive solo section, leaving the second violin to fade. During this solo passage, one may notice the climbing direction and dynamic changes of the line. Although pitches are indicated in the score, the durational elements are approximate and left to the player's discretion.

Example 2:

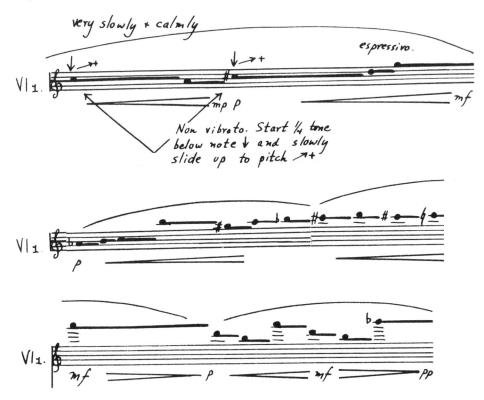

The solo lasts slightly longer than one minute and then a *pianissimo* chordal accompaniment begins.

Example 3:

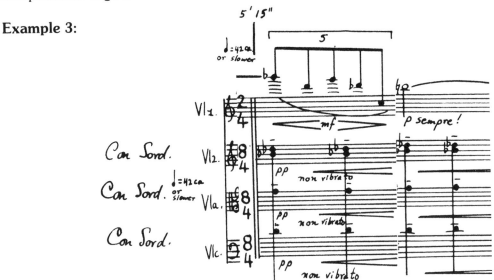

Notice the gradual *crescendo* and the 'breaking away' again of the solo violin. Joined again by the second violin, the duet continues with microtonal inflections in their respective lines.

Example 4:

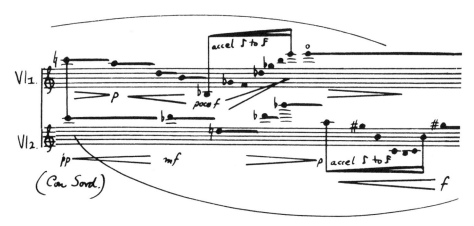

Once more, a chordal progression grows in intensity as it accompanies the solo violin. At this point, the composer requests a gradual sharpening of the pitch.

Example 5:

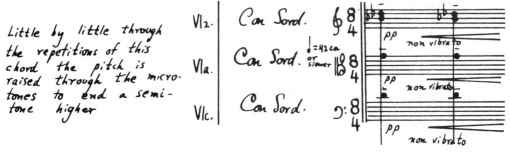

As the first violin and cello continue, a *pizzicato* accompaniment leads almost imperceptibly to the halfway point, ending the slow middle section. Here we notice a forceful chordal figure that is repetitive in nature.

Example 6:

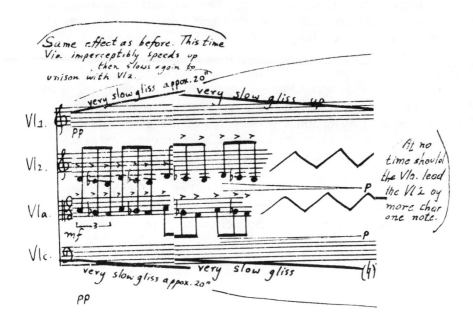

Same effect as before. This time Vla. imperceptibly speeds up then slows again to unison with Vl₂.

very slow gliss appox. 20"   very slow gliss up

At no time should the Vla. lead the Vl 2 by more than one note.

very slow gliss appox. 20"   very slow gliss

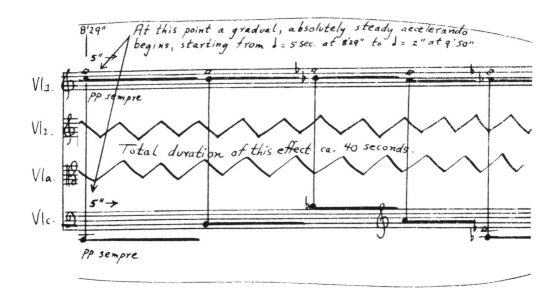

8'29"

At this point a gradual, absolutely steady accelerando begins, starting from ♩ = 5 sec. at 8'29" to ♩ = 2" at 9'50"

Total duration of this effect ca. 40 seconds.

PP sempre

Notice the sound effects of these next few pages in the score achieved through the use of upper harmonics, *glissandos,* double stopping, and unison. This unusual passage leads into the *cadenza* which begins with the cello. As each player (rising through from the lowest part) performs the cadential passages, the music is improvised. No specific notes are given — only the outline contours of each melodic line guide the direction and duration. One may notice the growing frenzy of the music and the punctuated sounds of the snapping chords. The momentary solo violin leads again to *tremolo* playing and a growing intensity. With a slight increase in tempo and a sharpening of the pitch, the motion of the music gradually subsides with periods of silence punctuated by loud snapping *pizzicato* chords.

This is music that defies tradition. Only through repeated exposure to the listening process can one hope to gain a greater understanding. However, the sounds that are produced are uniquely satisfying to those who will spend time and effort in developing an appreciation for such music.

Glossary

A Cappella   A choral performance without instrumental accompaniment.

Accidental   A sign which indicates the chromatic alteration of a single note.

Antiphonal   A term which originated from sacred music where the singers or performers responded from either side of the altar; meaning from either side and alternately from the choir.

Atonal   A term applied to twentieth-century music in which no tonal centre is apparent.

Augmentation   The lengthening of the note values of a melody.

Bimodality   A compositional device in twentieth-century music in which two different modes are employed simultaneously.

Bitonality   A compositional device in twentieth-century music in which two different tonalities are employed simultaneously.

Bridge passage   A musical link between two musical ideas.

Cadence   One of several chord progressions that may occur at the end of a phrase to give a feeling of finality or conclusion.

Cadenza   A florid passage which serves chiefly as a technical display for a solo performer — generally in the first movement of a concerto.

Canonic   An adjective of the noun canon; meaning in the form of imitation in which each part plays or sings the melody, entering at fixed intervals as in a round.

Cantata   A vocal composition of several sections for soloists, chorus, or both, with either a religious or secular text.

Cells   Short two-note and three-note progressions identified within a tone-row.

Chaconne   A variation form that is almost identical to that of the passacaglia. Originally a slow dance in triple time built from a repeated figure known as a ground bass.

Chorale   A congregational hymn of the German Lutheran Church.

Chordal   The style of the music is basically built from a chord structure or vertical alignment of notes.

Chromatic   Refers to the notes not normally associated with the diatonic notes of a major or minor scale, e.g. F# in the key of C major.

Coda   An Italian word meaning 'tail'; the concluding section of a composition, which is sometimes added to the main musical structure.

Concertino   A shorter and lighter type of concerto.

Concerto   A form in music which usually employs an instrumental soloist(s) and is accompanied by a symphony orchestra; normally in 3 movements.

211

Contrapuntal   This is the adjectival form of the term counterpoint, and refers to the linear progression of melodic strands within music of this nature.

Counterpoint   Music in which the chief interest lies in the satisfactory combination of various melodic strands.

Descant   A countermelody played or sung above the main melody of a song.

Diatonic   A seven-tone scale containing whole steps and half steps in a specific order.

Diminution   A shortening of note values of the original melody.

Dissonance   A combination of tones that creates a feeling of tension; the opposite of consonance.

Divertimento   A term used in the late 18th century and present times to denote a wide and varying range of instrumental combinations of a chamber nature; particularly for strings or wind instruments.

Divisi   Where the parts are divided; e.g. the first violins divide into 2 parts.

Dodecaphonism   Theorists of the Schoenberg or twelve-tone school prefer to call this method not a chromatic one, but 'dodecaphonic'.

Dominant   (1) The fifth scale tone above the tonic.   (2) the triad built on that tone.

Exposition   The first section of a composition, in which the basic themes are announced.

Fantasia   An instrumental composition which takes its form directly from the composer's imagination rather than from fixed rules.

Fragment   Usually a two-or three-note motive from a larger melodic entity.

Fragmentation   A compositional device utilizing fragments of a motive, or theme.

Fugue   A contrapuntal composition in which a subject is stated in a single voice (instrumental) and developed in an imitative style by two or more voices of equal importance.

Glissando   An effect produced by sliding the tone up or down.

Hexachord   A group of six consecutive tones, regarded as a unit for the purpose of creating unity in a composition.

Homophonic   Music that consists of a melodic line supported by a harmonic accompaniment.

Impressionism   A movement in the arts characterized by suggestion of subject matter by use of vague outline rather than by bold description.

Interval   The distance in pitch between two musical tones.

Inversion   Reversing the pitch direction of the tones of a melody; frequently used in twelve-tone music.

Libretto   The text used in vocal compositions.

Modal   Derived from the early modes which preceded the major and minor scales of earlier times.

Modulation   The harmonic process of changing from one key to another key during the course of a composition.

Motif   A short musical idea or melodic fragment of a theme.

Movement   The term is applied to separate divisions within a larger composition. For example, a symphony usually has four movements, whereas a concerto has three movements.

Muted   The use of a mute to quieten and alter the usual sound of an instrument.

Neo-classic   In music a 20th century movement marked by the return to the style of classical composers such as Johann Sebastian Bach.

Obbligato   An added part above the melody similar to a descant.

Ostinato   A clearly defined musical figure which is persistently repeated.

Passacaglia   This form originated as a key-board composition. The form usually employs an eight-measure ground bass in triple time which repeats. Over this bass foundation is built an ediface of harmonic and melodic material.

Pizzicato   A term used to indicate that the strings are to be plucked with the fingers instead of a bow.

Polyphonic   Denotes the style or texture of the music as horizontal or linear in nature rather than vertical or chordal.

Quartet   A group of four performers as in a string quartet.

Quintet   A group of five performers.

Recapitulation   The last section of a movement in which basic themes are restated and the entire movement is brought to a close.

Retrograde   A reversal of a melodic passage, beginning with the last note and ending with the first.

Retrograde Inversion   The playing or reading of a melody backwards and upside down at the same time.

Rhapsodic   Usually denotes a flowing melodic line somewhat ecstatic in nature; characteristically extravagant.

Ripieno   An Italian word used to designate the large or reinforcing group of instruments in the 18th century concerto grosso.

Rondo   A form consisting of a given theme with contrasting themes — for example, ABACABA.

Row (12-tone)   A series of tones, rather than a scale, on which a composition may be based.

Segments   Small units of two, three, or four notes within the larger context of a tone-row.

Serial   A term associated with twelve-tone music. A series of tones rather than a scale on which a composition is based.

Solo/tutti   The alternation of solo performer and instrumental group, usually in early concerti music.

Sonata   Since the classical era, the term usually has referred to a solo instrumental composition in three or four movements, the first of which may be in sonata form.

Sonata form   The name of a general musical form consisting of three major divisions: exposition, development, and recapitulation. Usually employed in the first movements of large symphonic compositions.

Spiccato   A term used to indicate a technique of bowing in which the bow is bounced on the strings.

Staccato   Detached, separated; with the sounding time of each note shortened.

Subject   In fugal writing, a theme which is heard alone at the beginning and then imitated by various voices or instruments.

Syncopation A rhythmic effect produced when the expected rhythm pattern is deliberately misplaced or upset from the strong beats in a measure to the weaker beats.

Ternary Three part form as in ABA design.

Timbre The particular tone quality of an instrument or group of instruments.

Toccata A composition originally for keyboard which demonstrated finger virtuosity. In free fantasia style.

Tonality Refers to the particular key centre in a composition.

Tone-row A prearranged order of the twelve tones of an octave. A tone-row serves as the basis for some types of twentieth century musical composition.

Transposition The writing or performing of a composition at a higher or lower pitch level than the original.

Variation The modification of a theme either melodically, rhythmically, or harmonically.

Whole tone scale Six tones which all lie one tone apart, e.g. c, d, e, f#, g#, a#.

Italian Terms

Accelerando	Faster by degrees
Adagio	Very slowly
Adagio sonante	Sounding very slowly
Affetuoso	With tenderness
Allegretto	Light and cheerful
Allegro	Quick, lively
Allegro e ritmico	Fast and rhythmical
Allegro con anima	Fast and with liveliness
Allegro con spirito	Quick with spirit
Andante	In moderate speed or tempo
Ben cantabile e marcata	Mark well the song-like melody
Ben pronunziata	Pronounced clearly and distinctly
Cantabile	Song-like, in a singing style
Con sordino	To be played with mutes
Con spirito	With spirit
Crescendo	Gradually becoming louder

Diminuendo	Decreasing the power or volume
Dolce	Sweetly
Duple	2 beats to a measure
Esaltato	Excitedly
Feroce	Fiercely, with ferocity
Fortissimo	Very loud
Inquieto	Restless, uneasy
Leggiero	In a light manner
Lento	In slow time
Ma molto leggiero	But very lightly
Marcato	Well marked or accentuated
Moderato	In moderate time
Molto piu mosso	With more movement
Molto tranquillo	Very peacefully
Mysterioso	Mysteriously
Piangendo	Despondingly, dolefully
Pianissimo	Very softly
Piu agitato	A more rapid agitated style
Piu Andante	A little more slowly
Poco a poco	Little by little
Poco largo	A little more slowly
Precipitando	In a hurried manner
Rallentando	Gradually slower
Risoluto	Resolutely
Scherzando	In a light, playful and sportive manner
Scherzo	Lively and playful
Simile	To continue in a similar manner
Soave	Softly, sweetly
Sonore	Sonorously or full toned
Staccatissimo	As staccato or detached as possible
Subito	Suddenly
Teneramente	Tenderly, delicately
Vigoroso	With energy and vigour
Vivace	Lively, quickly

Reference Notes

p. 3   Giles Bryant, "The Music of Healey Willan." *Musicanada,* Vol. 9 (March, 1968), p. 5.

p. 4   Andrée Desautels, "The History of Canadian Composition 1610-1967." *Aspects of Music in Canada* (Arnold Walter, editor), Toronto: University of Toronto Press (1969), p. 101.

p. 8   Udo Kasemets, "New Music." *The Canadian Music Journal,* Vol. 5, No. 2 (Winter, 1961), p. 49.

p. 17   Thomas Archer, "Claude Champagne." *The Canadian Music Journal,* Vol. 2, No. 2 (Winter, 1958), p. 3.

p. 18   Thomas Archer, "Claude Champagne." *The Canadian Music Journal,* Vol. 2, No. 2 (Winter, 1958), p. 4.

p. 18   Marvin Duchow, "Claude Champagne." *The Music Scene,* No. 243 (September-October, 1968), p. 7.

p. 19   Andrée Desautels, "The History of Canadian Composition 1610-1967." *Aspects of Music in Canada* (Arnold Walter, editor), Toronto: University of Toronto Press (1969), p. 108.

p. 21   Thomas Archer, "Claude Champagne." *The Canadian Music Journal,* Vol. 2, No. 2 (Winter, 1958), p. 9.

p. 24   Michael Olver, "Music Review." *The Montreal Star* quoted in *The Music Scene,* No. 248.

p. 24   Michael Olver, "Altitude." (Music Review), *The Montreal Star,* 1971.

p. 24   John Beckwith, "Perspectives." *The Canadian Music Journal,* Vol. 4, No. 4 (Summer, 1960), p. 45.

p. 28   Andrée Desautels, "The History of Canadian Composition 1610-1967." *Aspects of Music in Canada* (Arnold Walter, editor), Toronto: University of Toronto Press (1969), p. 108.

p. 28   Serge Garant, "Reviews." *The Canadian Music Journal,* Vol. 4, No. 1 (Autumn, 1959), p. 52.

p. 35   Godfrey Ridout, "Sir Ernest MacMillan: An Appraisal." *Music Across Canada,* Vol. 1, No. 6 (July-August, 1963), p. 32.

p. 49   Richard Savage, "Murray Adaskin: Composer, Professor, Gentleman." *The Canadian Composer/Le Compositeur Canadien,* No. 10 (September, 1966), p. 4.

p. 59   Kurt Stone, "Rondino for Nine Instruments." *The Musical Quarterly,* Vol. 53, No. 3 (July, 1967), p. 449.

p. 71   "Professor John Weinzweig: Important Musical Influence." *The Canadian Composer,* No. 14 (January, 1967), p. 40.

p. 71   June Champagne, "Interview: John Weinzweig." *The Canadian Composer,* No. 100 (April, 1975), pp. 26, 42.

p. 72   Udo Kasemets, "John Weinzweig." *The Canadian Music Journal,* Vol. 4, No. 4 (Summer, 1960), p. 14.

p. 73   Ken Winters, "Music Review." *The Toronto Telegram,* May 1, 1967.

p. 75   John Weinzweig, *Divertimento No. 3,* 1960. *Score,* Toronto: Leeds Music (Canada) Ltd.

p. 80   John Weinzweig, *Divertimento No. 5,* 1961. *Score,* Toronto: Leeds Music (Canada) Ltd.

p. 84   Kurt Stone, "Weinzweig's Woodwind Quintet," 1964. *The Musical Quarterly,* Vol. 53, No. 3 (July, 1967), p. 447.

p. 100   John Beckwith, "Jean Papineau-Couture." *The Canadian Music Journal,* Vol. 3, No. 2 (Winter, 1959), p. 7.

p. 101   Yolande Rivard, "Jean Papineau-Couture's Return to Tone Colour." *The Music Scene,* No. 254 (July-August, 1970), p. 4.

p. 101   John Beckwith, "Jean Papineau-Couture." *The Canadian Music Journal,* Vol. 3, No. 2 (Winter, 1959), p. 17.

p. 102   Eric McLean, "Music Review." *Montreal Star,* February 7th, 1973.

p. 103   John Beckwith, "Reviews." *The Canadian Music Journal,* Vol. 1, No. 4 (Summer, 1957), p. 49.

p. 103   Andrée Desautels, "The History of Canadian Composition 1610-1967." *Aspects of Music in Canada* (Arnold Walter, editor), Toronto: University of Toronto Press (1969), p. 118.

p. 120   Madeleine Bernier, "Music Review." *The Winnipeg Tribune,* January 23, 1972.

p. 120   Max Wyman, "Music Review." *The Vancouver Sun,* quoted in *The Music Scene,* No. 270 (March-April, 1973), p. 16.

p. 120   Peter Garvie, "Robert Turner." *The Music Scene,* No. 245 (January-February, 1969), p. 9.

p. 140   Michael Schulman, "Harry Freedman." *The Canadian Composer,* No. 96 (December, 1974), p. 8.

p. 140   Bryan Wilkinson, "Harry Freedman: An Exciting Composer." *The Canadian Composer,* No. 17 (April, 1967), p. 4.

p. 141   Michael Schulman, "Harry Freedman." *The Canadian Composer,* No. 96 (December, 1974), p. 8.

p. 144   Felix Aprahamian, "Music Review." *London Sunday Times,* November, 1965.

p. 145   "Ovation for Canadian Abroad with Toronto Symphony." *The Canadian Composer,* No. 4 (December, 1965), p. 32.

p. 151   Kurt Stone, *The Musical Quarterly,* Vol. 53, No. 3 (July, 1967), p. 447.

p. 157   Harry Freedman, *Tangents.* (Score), Willowdale, Ontario: Leeds Music (Canada) Ltd. (1971), p. 2.

p. 171   Udo Kasemets, "Pierre Mercure." *The Music Scene,* No. 246 (March-April, 1969), p. 10.

p. 171   Michael Grobin, "Our Composers on Microgroove — Part II." *Musicanada,* No. 27 (March, 1970), p. 10.

p. 180   Udo Kasemets, "New Music." *The Canadian Music Journal,* Vol. 5, No. 2 (Winter, 1961), p. 52.

p. 189   Suzanne Ball, "Murray Schafer — Composer, Teacher and Author." *The Music Scene,* No. 253 (May-June, 1970), p. 7.

p. 190   Peter Such, "R. Murray Schafer." *Soundprints,* Toronto: Clarke, Irwin and Company Ltd. (1972), p. 133.

p. 191   "R. Murray Schafer," BMI Canada Limited, Brochure, n.d.

p. 192   Udo Kasemets, "R. Murray Schafer." *Contemporary Canadian Composers,* Toronto: Oxford University Press (Canadian Branch), 1975, p. 200.

p. 194   R. Murray Schafer, "Threnody: A Religious Piece of Our Time." *Music AGO/RCCO Magazine,* Vol. 4, No. 5 (May, 1970), p. 34.

p. 194   Robert Sunter, "Review of Threnody." *The Vancouver Sun,* quoted in *R. Murray Schafer,* Toronto: BMI Canada Limited, Brochure, n.d.

p. 201   R. Murray Schafer, *Epitaph for Moonlight.* Toronto: Berandol Music Limited, 1968.

p. 201   Elmer Iseler, "Epitaph for Moonlight." *The Music Scene,* No. 268 (November-December, 1972), p. 15.

p. 204   Lloyd Dykk, "Review of R. Murray Schafer's String Quartet." Quoted in *The Music Scene,* No. 256 (November-December, 1970), p. 11.

Bibliography

For teachers and students anxious to pursue the study of Canadian music in greater depth, there exists a wide range of published articles and books. Unfortunately, many of these resources are either out of print, or lie hidden in obscure journals difficult for most people to locate. From approximately two thousand bibliographic entries known to the author, a few of the basic and more easily obtained readings are selected and listed under appropriate headings. It is hoped that these resources will provide additional reference for readers, and aid in the search for material that is useful for education.

Bibliographical

Bio-Bibliographical Finding List of Canadian Musicians (2nd edition). Ottawa: Canadian Association of Music Libraries, 1974.

Bradley, Ian L. *A Selected Bibliography of Musical Canadiana.* Toronto: GLC Publishers Limited, 1976.

Canadian Broadcasting Corporation. *The Canadian Collection/La Collection Canadienne.* Catalogue of Recordings, 1975.

Canadian Music Library Association. *A Selected List of Music Reference Materials* (revised edition), 1969.

Creative Canada (2 Vols.). *A Biographical Dictionary of 20th Century Creative and Performing Artists.* Reference Division of McPherson Library, University of Victoria; Toronto: University of Toronto Press, 1971-72.

Fowke, Edith and Barbara Cass-Beggs. *A Reference List on Canadian Folk Music* (revised edition). Montreal: Canadian Folk Music Society, 1973.

Hall, Frederick A. et al. *A Basic Bibliography of Musical Canadiana* (mimeographed). University of Toronto Library, 1970.

Kallmann, Helmut (editor). *Catalogue of Canadian Composers.* Toronto: Canadian Broadcasting Corporation, 1952.

Kasemets, Udo (editor). *Canavangard, Music of the 1960's, Catalogue and Biographies.* Toronto: BMI Canada, 1967.

MacMillan, Keith and John Beckwith (editors). *Contemporary Canadian Composers.* Toronto: Oxford University Press (Canadian Branch), 1975.

Radio Canada International. *Catalogue.* Recordings produced by the Transcription Service of Radio Canada International, May, 1974.

Biographical

Canadian Broadcasting Corporation, International Service. *Thirty-four Biographies of Canadian Composers.* Reprint, St. Clair Shores, Mich.: Scholarly Press, 1972.

McCready, Louise G. *Famous Musicians: MacMillan, Johnson, Pelletier, Willan.* Toronto: Clarke, Irwin and Company Limited, 1957.

Such, Peter. *Soundprints.* Toronto: Clarke, Irwin and Company Limited, 1972.

Compositional

Beckwith, John. "Composers in Toronto and Montreal." *University of Toronto Quarterly,* Vol. 26 (October, 1956), pp. 47-69.

George, Graham. "Canada's Music — 1955, an Attempt to Assess the Quality of Contemporary Composition." *Culture,* Vol. 16 (March, 1955), pp. 51-65.

Schafer, R. Murray. "The Limits of Nationalism in Canadian Music." *Tamarack Review,* Vol. 18 (Winter, 1961), pp. 71-78.

Educational

Adaskin, Harry. "Music and the University." *Canadian Music Journal,* Vol. 1, No. 1 (1956), pp. 30-36.

Adaskin, Murray. "The University in Audience Training." *Music Across Canada,* Vol. 1, No. 5 (June, 1963), pp. 16-18.

Bradley, Ian L. "Canadian Music: Resources for the Classroom Teacher." *The British Columbia Music Educator,* Vol. 18, No. 2 (Spring, 1975), pp. 35-43.

Bradley, Ian L. "Canadian Music: Stranger in the Classroom." *The British Columbia Music Educator,* Vol. 17, No. 1 (January, 1974), pp. 25-28.

McKellar, Donald A. "A New Dimension for Canadian Music Education: Sociomusicology." *The British Columbia Music Educator,* Vol. 15, No. 1 (October, 1971), pp. 21-26.

Mills, Isabelle. "Canadian Music for Young Listeners." *The Canadian Music Educator,* Vol. 14, No. 3 (Spring, 1973), pp. 12-16.

Nourse, Nancy. "Canadian Music in the Canadian Classroom." *The Canadian Music Educator,* Vol. 16, No. 3 (Spring, 1975), pp. 5-15.

Walter, Arnold. "The Growth of Music Education." *Aspects of Music in Canada* (ed. by Arnold Walter), Toronto: University of Toronto Press (1969), pp. 247-287.

Ethnomusicological

Carlisle, Roxane C. *Folk Music in Canada — 1974.* Ottawa: Canadian Centre for Folk Culture Studies, National Museums of Canada, 1974.

Barbeau, Marius and Helen Creighton. "The Rediscovery of Folk Music." *Canadian Geographical Journal,* Vol. 84, No. 3 (March, 1972), pp. 82-91.

Creighton, Helen. "Canada's Maritime Provinces — An Ethnomusicological Survey." *Ethnomusicology,* Vol. 16, No. 3 (September, 1972), pp. 404-414.

Densmore, Frances. *Music of the Indians of British Columbia.* Bureau of American Ethnology, Anthropological Papers, Bulletin 136, Washington, 1943; Reprint, New York: Da Capo Press, 1972.

Ethnomusicology. Journal of the Society for Ethnomusicology. Canadian Number: Vol. 16, No. 3 (September, 1972).

Fowke, Edith. "Anglo-Canadian Folksong: A Survey." *Ethnomusicology,* Vol. 16, No. 3 (September, 1972), pp. 335-350.

Fowke, Edith. "Folk Songs in Ontario." *Canadian Literature,* Vol. 16 (1963), pp. 28-42.

Halpern, Ida. *Indian Music of the Pacific Northwest Coast.* Notes for two Ethnic Folkways 12" volumes, FE 4523, 1967. 26 pp., and FE 4524, 1974.

Peacock, Kenneth. "Folk and Aboriginal Music." *Aspects of Music in Canada* (ed. by Arnold Walter), Toronto: University of Toronto Press (1969), pp. 62-89.

Thomas, Philip J. "B.C. Songs." *British Columbia. Library Quarterly,* Vol. 26 (July, 1962), pp. 15-29.

Historical

Amtmann, Willy. *Music in Canada.* Toronto: Collier-Macmillan, Canada Limited, 1975.

Kallmann, Helmut. *A History of Music in Canada 1534-1914.* Toronto: University of Toronto Press, 1960.

Littler, William. "A History of Canadian Music on Thirteen Records." *The Canadian Composer/Le Compositeur* Canadien, No. 98 (February, 1975), pp. 24-28.

MacMillan, Sir Ernest C. (editor). *Music in Canada.* Toronto: University of Toronto Press, 1955.

Palk, Helen. "The Music Makers." *The Book of Canadian Achievement,* Toronto: J. M. Dent (1951), pp. 203-34.

Ross, M. (editor). *The Arts in Canada: A Stock-taking at Mid-Century.* Toronto: Macmillan, 1958.

Spell, L. "Music in New France in the Seventeenth Century." *Canadian Historical Review,* Vol. 8 (June, 1927), pp. 119-31.

Walter, Arnold (editor). *Aspects of Music in Canada.* Toronto: University of Toronto Press, 1969.

Organizational

Beaudet, J. M. "The National Arts Centre." *The Music Scene,* No. 244 (November-December, 1968), pp. 7-8.

Cozens, John. "The Canadian Music Council." *The Canadian Music Educator,* Vol. 13, No. 3 (Spring, 1972), p. 14.

Halpenny, Mary. "The N.Y.O. Inside Out." *The Canadian Music Educator,* Vol. 15, No. 3 (Spring, 1974), pp. 3-10.

Kallmann, Helmut. "Music Division, National Library of Canada." *The Music Scene* (May-June, 1971), p. 4.

MacMillan, Keith. "National Organizations." *Aspects of Music in Canada* (ed. by Arnold Walter), Toronto: University of Toronto Press (1969), pp. 288-318.

Schabas, Ezra. "National Youth Orchestra — 1965." *The Canadian Music Educator* (October-November, 1965), pp. 42-45.

Discography

The following works have been recorded either on commercial labels or may be found in the Canadian Broadcasting Corporation's catalogue, *The Canadian Collection.* To obtain CBC records it is necessary to address all orders or enquiries to: CBC Publications, Box 500, Station 'A', Toronto, Ontario M5W 1E6

Willan, Healey

An Apostrophe To The Heavenly Hosts. Gloria-Melbourne SMLP 4030.

Pianoforte Concerto in C minor. CBC, SM-205.

Passacaglia and Fugue in E minor. CBC, SM-202; Columbia, Canada, ML 6198 and MS 6798.

Champagne, Claude

Symphonie gaspésienne. CBC Radio Canada International, RCI-216.

Altitude for Chorus and Orchestra. CBC Radio Canada International, RCI-179.

String Quartet. CBC Radio Canada International, RCI-143.

MacMillan, Sir Ernest

Two Sketches for Strings, On French Canadian Airs. Canadian Music in the Twentieth Century — Columbia, MS 6962; Deutsche Grammophon SLPM 139900 (Quartet version); Odyssey Y 31993.

String Quartet in C minor. Deutsche Grammophon SLPM 139900.

Adaskin, Murray

Rondino for Nine Instruments. CBC Radio Canada International Recording, RCI-215 Stereo.

Diversion for Orchestra (An Entertainment). CBC Radio Canada International Recording, SM-294 Stereo.

Sonata for Violin and Piano. CBC Radio Canada Recording, SM-211 Stereo.

Weinzweig, John

Divertimento No. 3. CBC SM-15.

Woodwind Quintet. Radio Canada International Recording, RCI-218 Stereo.

Divertimento No. 5. Radio Canada International Recording, RCI-292 Stereo.

Papineau-Couture, Jean

Concerto for Piano and Orchestra. L'Orchestre de Radio-Canada a Montreal, Radio Canada International Service Recording, RCI-235 Stereo.

Pièce concertante No. 3. Radio Canada International Service Recording, RCI-293 Stereo.

Psaume 150. Radio Canada International Service Recording, Programme 128.

Turner, Robert

Variations and Toccata. Radio Canada International Recording, RCI-215 Stereo.

Serenade for Woodwind Quintet. CBC SM-139 Stereo.

Opening Night — A Theatre Overture. Radio Canada International Service Recording, Programme 179.

Freedman, Harry

Variations for flute, oboe and harpsichord. CBC Radio Canada International Recording, RCI-219 Stereo.

Images. The Toronto Symphony, Columbia, MS 6962 Stereo.

Tangents. The Toronto Symphony World Records 477-4001.

Mercure, Pierre

Cantate pour une joie. CBC Radio Canada International, RCI-155.

Divertissement. CBC Radio Canada International, RCI-154.

Triptyque. Canadian Music in the Twentieth Century — Columbia MS 6962; Odyssey Y 31993.

Schafer, R. Murray

Threnody. Melbourne SMLP 4017.

Epitaph for Moonlight. Melbourne SMLP 4017 and CBC SM-274.

String Quartet (1970). CBC Radio Canada International Recording, RCI-353 Stereo; Melbourne SMLP 4026 Stereo.